Mission Next

Successfully transitioning from
the military to the civilian workforce

DR. JOHN WOJCIK

Colonel (USA, Retired)

&

KIMBERLIE ENGLAND

MISSION NEXT

Successfully transitioning from the military to the civilian workforce

CONTENTS

PROLOGUE

B loomberg recently reported that the Department of Defense (DoD) needs to recruit over 150,000 service members each year to reach the targeted active-duty end strength for the Army, Navy, Air Force, and Marine Corps. To make that happen, the DoD spends a little over $7 billion each year to maintain its cadre of talented recruiters to find civilians and turn them into service members.

While your branch of service has spent an incredible amount of time and money to recruit you into active duty, it will spend far less to integrate you back into the civilian world. Talk to someone you know who has recently transitioned to their first civilian job. As of 2014, the federal government was running eighty-five different programs to help veterans transition. Eighty-five! Yet, the Government Accountability Office found that most of those programs had only limited success.

Why Should You Read This Book?

We spent two years intensely researching why veterans leave their first jobs. We read the books, articles, and research so you don't have to. We even did a formal research study to gather first-hand accounts about why veterans leave. At the end of 2021, John defended his doctoral dissertation on the topic of why military officers leave their civilian jobs. The process was the culmination of almost six years of doctoral studies, document reviews, research, and formally presenting and defending the work. This led to our desire to publish a book to help transitioning veterans by providing a toolkit that you can reference as you pass through each phase of the transition.

Most importantly, you should read this book because it will increase your chances at achieving a smooth transition and finding a job that fits. It's a resource that covers every aspect of your transition from the military to the civilian workforce. *Mission Next* provides checklists and tips to make your journey easier. It also uses plain English to explain complicated concepts, such as civilian pay and benefits, so you can make informed decisions about your employment options.

When we talked to veterans about their transition, they told us, "It's like I was the first person to ever retire." Joining the service is easy. Leaving is a whole lot harder. During your first year in service, you spent months learning your first military occupational skill—and you spent years refining and expanding those skills. Becoming an expert didn't happen overnight; it took time and hard work. This next transition in your life requires dedication and commitment so you don't become a statistic. The numbers are shocking. Close to 65% of active-duty veterans leave their first civilian jobs within 24 months—and those are the ones who find a job quickly when they get out.

You need to rediscover who you are, write a resume that civilians can understand, find a job that fits, and learn how to operate in your new civilian work environment. You've received your new assignment—your next mission. Welcome to *Mission Next*.

Getting Professional Help

Adjusting to the change from military life to the civilian workplace can be extremely stressful for the service member and his or her family. While *Mission Next* is designed to help you as you transition to the civilian workplace, it is not a replacement for professional support. If you or a family member starts having trouble coping with this transition, you (or your family member) may find it helpful to speak to a therapist to become better able to adjust to the things they cannot control.

The Department of Defense does an amazing job in making it easy to connect veterans with mental health professionals. Don't believe us? A senior officer who retired recently told us he spent "over a day and a half" calling different therapists in his area to schedule an appointment for his teenage children. Call after call after call, he was told the providers didn't take Tricare or weren't taking new clients. But with one call to Military OneSource, he found himself talking to a real person whose job it was to connect his family with mental health assistance. The resource provider called a provider with him still on the phone, and together they coordinated a plan for his family's mental health care. The number for Military OneSource is 800-342-9647.

The views presented are those of the authors and do not necessarily represent the views of the DoD or its components.

1

UNDERSTANDING WHY VETERANS LEAVE THEIR FIRST JOB

This book is not designed to tell you what you're going to face when you transition without providing solutions. It's also not going to come up with the answers for you. That's because everyone's path is different and some things in life are hard. Challenging. Demanding. What you're about to experience—the military to civilian transition process—is not an easy thing to go through. You can, however, have a truly successful transition if you take the time to prepare and get yourself ready.

This book is also not simply one person's perspective of what happened to them upon their retirement or ETS. The bookshelves are full of those accounts, often written by someone famous or high-ranking. They may even have a great headshot on the front cover. While reading about someone's personal experiences may be helpful, this book is supported by academic theory and peer-reviewed research. Wait, don't run away. This isn't a book of philosophy and statistics. It's a book that uses research and theory to help make transitioning as painless as possible. It's going to get you where you want to be as you step into the civilian workforce.

This book is full of thought-provoking questions and exercises. If you want to make the most of this book—and have the best chance of a smooth transition—do the exercises. Every one of them. This might mean that you will have to work for weeks, or maybe even months, but it'll be worth it.

Why Did You Join the Military?

Put yourself back to the point when you first thought, "I think I want to join the military." It may have been only three or six years ago, or maybe more than twenty years have gone by since you made that decision. Regardless of how long ago it's been, write down the first five reasons that come to mind when you reflect on your reasons for joining the military.

WHY I JOINED THE MILITARY?
1.
2.
3.
4.
5.

It doesn't matter if you write a few words, or a few sentences for each reason. Focus on what words come to your mind. You'll use this information in Chapter 3 as you begin to identify your values and define your personal vision.

The Statistics on Leaving the Military

The best way to understand why veterans leave their first job is to examine the statistics. Over 200,000 service members leave active duty every year. To help personalize that number, consider how many people are working in your unit right now. Are there 10, 50, 300, or even 1,000? Now think about how many units like yours leave active duty every single day. It's really a staggering amount of people that are faced with the challenges of transitioning into the civilian workforce. Keep in mind that for every service member that leaves, there are spouses, kids, step-kids, parents (and maybe a pet or two) who are transitioning too. All those moving parts are each going to behave in their own distinct way. You won't be able to control all of it, but by preparing yourself as much as possible, you can limit the chaos that is likely to swirl around the decision to leave the military.

Some service members figure out how to smoothly transition with limited support, while others most certainly do not. As mentioned in the prologue, the Department of Defense and your branch of service worked hard to get you to enlist. They spent tens of thousands of dollars to get you to leave your comfortable, civilian world to wear a camouflage uniform to work every day. Your branch of service will try to help you transition, but keep in mind that the people working with you through this process will likely only be able to share their own personal experiences of what happened in their lives when they left active duty. That's why it's up to you to create your own personalized roadmap to transitioning. Your success in navigating this transition is almost entirely up to you.

We've established that each day, the equivalent of an entire crew of four fast attack submarines (around 550 per day) leaves active duty. Once those submariners leave service, 46% of them will still be looking for their first job after one year. The ones who do secure a civilian job will end up leaving those civilian organizations at incredibly high rates—rates that far exceed civilian turnover rates.

In the civilian world, around 19% of employees leave their jobs within the first year of being hired. Turnover rates for veterans are noticeably higher. Studies show that between 54% and 65% of veterans will leave their first civilian job by the end of their second year. Officers tend to stay in place a little longer than enlisted service members.

- **Year One.** 26.7% of officers reported leaving while 48% of enlisted service members reported leaving in that first year.

- **Year Two.** 26% of officers reported leaving while 20% of enlisted service members reported leaving in that second year.

It is difficult to ignore the staggering difference between how quickly former military members leave their first jobs compared to the civilian turnover rates. Civilian organizations repeatedly share how much they want to hire veterans. Government analysis and research studies back up this claim. Study after study confirms that businesses value veterans and want to hire them. The dissertation pointed to a long list of skills and values that civilian organizations desperately want including "sense of duty, commitment, dedication, selfless service, and leadership." They want you and you want to work for those organizations. So, what's the problem? It turns out that the answer is a little complicated, but with the right tools, you'll be off to a good start.

The Gap between Military and Civilian Life

Look back at your notes from a couple pages earlier where you were asked to jot down the reasons you joined the armed services in the first place. That was how you felt before you signed up for duty and laced up your first pair of boots. After that, you spent the next [insert your number of years of service] years training, fighting, learning, and leading with people who were just like you. They lived in barracks and off-base housing just like you did. They PCS'd every couple years, which meant finding new schools, discovering the new local hangouts, and even making new friends. While you were on active duty, you constantly learned new skills and built-up your standing or credibility both as a service member and as a leader.

This is your "normal." Every day, you got up, did PT or PRT with your team, put on the uniform, worked, and maybe hit the commissary on the way home. Everyone in your world was pretty much like you. Even your spouse and kids spoke the language and followed the behaviors without need for translation. You didn't have to explain why you needed to get out of your car at 1700 to salute the flagpole before you zipped off base to your HOR. Everybody just got it. It's not going to be like that where you're going. We're talking about your next mission: *Mission Next*.

Making a Plan—a Real Plan—for Change

Research shows that any time a human undergoes a significant transition, that transition requires the human to adapt to their new surroundings in such a way they can understand or at least coexist with the other humans in their new environment. In other words, change requires that you adapt. You've done this before though. Maybe you were in service when the DoD made "enhancements" to its Defense Travel System, which drove some service members crazy as they needed to figure out how to upload their travel vouchers and receipts and re-learn how to book a flight. Maybe you had to work through the Army's new personnel management systems that merged human resource data, medical information, and performance evaluation systems with less than stellar results. Change can be painful, and adaptation can take a lot of work. During these transitions, people make mistakes and that's okay. The key is to give the change the attention it deserves. Studies show that creating a deliberate plan to address the change helps humans do a better job in navigating their way through transitions.

Understanding Capital

Social scientists have studied how humans experience change for well over a hundred years. This means you don't have to spend time studying change theory, and this book will help you understand what's really going on as you navigate the social change.

When you were at basic training or in your officers commissioning course, you were indoctrinated into a new culture. You stopped being a civilian and became a service member. Change happened. There were times when you didn't understand how your new society worked, or how you would learn all those new skills that were required. But you did. You pushed through all the uncertainty and figured it all out.

In this military culture, you had a rank and understood where you fit into the military organization. As you learned new skills, earned rank, and developed your leadership skills, you were developing something called "capital." You experienced increases in all different types of capital as you developed into your new, military self. Here are a couple examples of "capital." You developed…

- **Social capital** when you became an E-7 or a field grade officer—instant "street cred."

- **Intellectual capital** when you became a subject matter expert and everyone started coming to you with questions about increasing signal strength.

- **Financial capital** by saving money in your Thrift Savings Plan or expanding your investments. Note: Financial capital can ease the transition by giving you more time to find that perfect job.

The point is this: you've spent your entire career developing your capital and that capital typically increases as you learned new skills and earned new rank. In Chapter 9, you will learn more about how to take some of this capital and maximize it in the civilian workplace.

Understanding Field and Habitus

You also operated within certain social sets in your new active-duty world. At work, during physical training, and at other military events, you operated within your military "field." Outside work, you might have enjoyed civilianized hobbies like soccer, bar trivia, or running marathons. Maybe you were active in your church. All these are examples of your ability to live and coexist with other people in different fields.

From E-1 to E-7 or O-1 through O-6 or CW-1 through CW-5, you started doing things a certain way in various situations. For example, you learned how much water you could drink before standing in a long formation without having to squirm your way through it. You knew to bring a carabiner with you before getting on a helicopter to make sure your ruck sack made the whole trip. You made check lists and maybe encouraged your kids to adapt to your "more organized" way of thinking. You were developing something called a "habitus."

In your military world—also called your field—you did things a certain way—also called your habitus. Your ability to get things done depended on how much capital you had accumulated. Consider these examples. A Colonel orders a Major to move-up the time of departure, "Roger Ma'am; got it." Boom, capital made that happen. A First Sergeant tells an Army Lieutenant, "Sir, I really don't think that's a great idea." Capital will make that Lieutenant take another look.

More than Pay and Benefits

What does any of that have to do with why veterans leave their first civilian jobs at such high rates? You've learned that capital affects your ability to get things done. Transitioning to the civilian world will have a serious impact on your capital unless you can figure out a way to transfer some of it. The more capital you take with you, the easier it will be for you to fit in and interact with others so you can get done what you want to get done. As you continue to read through the chapters in *Mission Next*—and do the exercises—you will learn many things that will help you in this goal.

It's important to remember this as you start preparing for your transition. It will help you combat the myth that your job selection should be based on pay and benefits. In other words, people will tell you to take the job where the total compensation is the highest. But is that right for you? Some surveys suggested that 65% of service members thought that pay and benefits were the reasons that they left their first civilian jobs in their first 24 months. The dissertation research resulted in different conclusions. Why is this? It's easier for a veteran to tell their family and friends that they left a position because the pay was lousy. It's harder to do a self-assessment and tell your family and friends that you left because "they" (your boss and coworkers) didn't understand you or think like you—that you didn't fit in, but that's what's really happening. Veterans leave because they picked a job that wasn't a good fit for them.

Consider asking this question to an audience of civilian employees: "What would I have to pay you to leave your spouse and children and your warm bed to fly overseas and spend a year in a combat zone, living in a tent, eating cold food, and taking cold showers, all while people are actively trying to kill you?" Most civilians would answer that there's no amount of money that would incentivize them to make that choice. But for you, things were different—and in some ways, they still are. You joined the service understanding that you would endure incredible hardships and potentially risk death or serious injury. So, honestly, you're not going to leave your first civilian job because someone in another company is willing to pay you 5% more for you to do the same job at their company. You were the one on an aircraft carrier in the middle of an upset ocean or standing on a hilltop on a border with zero sleep and a hungry belly.

Veterans leave civilian organizations because the service member is unable to mesh/conform/synch with their new civilian world—with their new civilian job. Being able to understand who you are is paramount to your ability to smooth out the bumps when you navigate your transition from active duty to your first civilian job. Put in the work. Assemble the plans. Your transition can be successful.

Taking Control of Your Transition

As mentioned in the prologue, this book is the culmination of a lifetime's worth of work in helping veterans and advocating for them in the court system, the legislature, and even with the Secretary of Defense's office. You will see references to published research and to the peer-reviewed research study that was the basis for the doctoral dissertation. Transitioning from the military into the civilian workforce can be separated into three phases.

- **Phase 1: Rediscovering who you are.** This book will guide you through the process and it's not nearly as painful as you think. You may even find the exercises in this book rather enlightening. Again, you'll only get results if you put in the work through completing the exercises and questionnaires.

- **Phase 2: Translating your military experience.** Research shows that there is disconnect between how the service members describe their military experience and the skills civilian employers are looking for (even though there could be a close match in those two areas). Studies also show that once veterans land their first civilian job, they struggle in being able to communicate with their managers and coworkers. Chapter 5 will explain how learning to speak the language—the civilian language—will increase your chances of securing your dream job and keeping it.

- **Phase 3: Understanding civilian work culture**. Organizational culture refers to the beliefs and behaviors that determine how an organization's employees and management interact. By understanding culture, you can leverage your military capital (that is, skills, education, training, and experiences that you gained while serving in the military). Because you don't get to walk around with your rank in your back pocket in the civilian world, it's important to ensure that your military capital is valued by your managers and coworkers.

2

PREPARING FOR CHANGE

You know this transition is going to be a real change. This is a no-kidding, preparation-needed, attention-required change in your life. So, you can't think of this change as merely checking the boxes and moving forward. Before you begin to work on your vision for post-military life, it's important to spend a little time understanding how people move through personal change and transition so you can be successful on your *Mission Next*.

The good thing is that social scientists have been studying the idea of personal change for quite a few years, and there are a couple of pretty amazing theories (or SOPs) you can use to help get the process started. This chapter will provide an overview of some of those theories so you can pick and choose what elements will help you push forward.

Before we talk about "change theory," let's reflect on your experiences with change. Do you remember when you got your first performance review? For you, this likely happened within several weeks after you went to basic training. While someone like you carried the unit's insignia or guide-on to all the different places you went to train, your drill sergeants let you know how you were doing on a pretty regular basis. This may have been your first introduction to the peer review process. Similarly, cadets in ROTC, OCS, and at the commissioning academies are constantly reviewed by their peers and by the cadre. They get rated on a daily basis and are consistently compared to what the cadre wants to see in an officer, and to the other pool of cadets who are competing for their grade/rank/scores. These reviews drive performance and encourage people to excel by recognizing where they are now and where they want to be.

It's also likely that the first time you were reviewed by another service member—whether it was a drill sergeant, a black hat, or a cadre—it felt pretty uncomfortable. Maybe their comments even stung a little. Maybe your view of yourself might not match what your cadre was seeing in you. Maybe you got amazing grades in high school or college, but you completely screwed up your first assignment at your military certification school. When those things happen, it really messes with the perception of how you see yourself compared to how others see you.

In the next chapter, the "military you" will complete a situation report on where you are right now. You will also spend some time identifying where you might want to go. These two pieces fit together into the place where Intentional Change Theory starts.

Intentional Change Theory

Don't think about a "theory" as some PhD's stuffy idea of putting all their research into page after page of stuff you need to learn. Instead, look at "theory" as an SOP that can help you get from point A to point B in the quickest way with the minimum amount of effort. Use all that PhD power to your advantage. They did the research and you're just walking through their SOP.

There are a bunch of different change theories out there, but there's one that stands out for people like you who are about to tackle the military to civilian change process. It's called the Intentional Change Theory and it's been taught for years by some amazing talent at Case Western Reserve University. What you need to know right now is the Intentional Change Theory takes place in four key steps:

1. Defining your Ideal Self and Personal Vision

2. Identifying your Real Self

3. Setting your goals for learning

4. Experimenting and practicing the changes you've identified

If you follow these steps—and are honest with yourself—you'll be well on your way to embracing the changes you need to not only succeed but excel.

Defining your Ideal Self and Personal Vision

Step one is fun. This is the step for the dreamer that lies deep inside you. Who do you want to be? What things do you want to get out of life? What's important to you? All those things drive your ability, or your willingness, to make choices in life that will align with your core values so you can be happy. Keep in mind that if you pick a job that you love, or move somewhere you really want to live, you are on a path that aligns with your ideal self—the person you really want to be.

The next chapter will guide you through some exercises that will help you articulate what you need to be happy. Most people don't spend enough time on this first phase. Hopefully it will be cathartic. It also may be just a bit painful if you discover that your goals, beliefs, and values didn't synch all that well with what you were doing in the military for the last six or twelve or twenty years. That's okay. It's never too late to get started.

Identifying your Real Self

If you look back to your first day or week of active duty, your version and perception of yourself in no way matched what your cadre or supervisors thought of you. You thought you were in great shape and were super smart. They thought you needed to run a little more and talk a whole lot less, and they most certainly told you about it.

You need to be able to "see yourself" for any real change to occur. "Seeing yourself" means understanding what other people see—the good and the bad—in you. There are many different ways to find out how others see you. The Army experimented with a 360° assessment model several years ago. The model asked peers, subordinates, and supervisors to fill out some online assessment tools to assess how they saw each service member as a leader. Though it was a great idea, nobody actually completed the assessments. It was easy to click a couple boxes on their Army evaluation form to bypass the 360° assessment tool. It's a shame because in the civilian world, 360° assessments are frequently used by businesses. They can help the organization assess the quality of incoming talent, or whether someone should be promoted or given advanced responsibilities.

There are a handful of places where you can arrange to have your own 360° assessment completed. As you review the options, make sure the information is easy to read and will help you see yourself as you are so you can do what you need to do to become more competitive in the civilian world. Most of those assessments can be done for less than $300. If you want to explore some of the online resources, you can find a host of great quality assessments with a simple internet search. Just be sure to let your coworkers and supervisors know that you're doing the assessments before the online services start sending out e-mails with links to complete your 360° assessments.

Another option is to complete your own self-assessment by using some tools that will help you self-reflect. You've likely heard of the Myers Briggs assessment tool. The Army used that tool for several years during Intermediate Leadership Education (ILE) courses, which you needed to complete to make O-5. Search the Internet and find a tool that works best for you. Just keep in mind that you're the one doing the assessment and that your bias may not give you a clear picture of how others view you.

Identifying your Real Self will improve your ability to engage with your civilian peers and subordinates, which deeply impacts your ability to succeed. The trick is being open to seeing yourself how others see you and being honest about your best attributes and flaws. If you aren't able to go through this step, you might struggle in the next phase, which involves building a training roadmap so you can move toward becoming your ideal self.

Setting Goals for Learning

Once you understand how other people see you—your Real Self—and have a better handle on the person you want to become—your Ideal Self—you can start filling in the gaps between the two. How do you do that? Think back to the first time you had to conduct your first military endeavor. Maybe you needed to move a platoon of soldiers from the motor pool to the range and back. How did you do it? You took your commander's orders, read them, and figured out how to have enough beans, bullets, and fuel to make it out there and back. You briefed your personnel and made sure they knew what you were asking them to do. Then, you executed the plan and made constant adjustments to make sure it all got done. See—you've done all this before.

The next chapter will guide you through some exercises that will enable you to build your personal learning goal sheet. It also has examples to help you form a picture of what yours might look like. To give you a preview, assume there's an artilleryman who wants to become a shop foreman in a manufacturing facility. What does that artilleryman need to know to become super competitive during the job interview? That person's thought process might look something like this:

- What are the manufacturing trends in this industry?

- Are there any certifications or training classes I can complete to make me more competitive on how to manufacture stuff?

- What kind of things are supervisors doing to manage their personnel in this manufacturing business?

- Who can I talk with to learn more about what supervisors in this industry do?

- Which companies near my ideal location have these types of jobs?

- What kind of civilian education do supervisors have in this industry?

- How many years of experience do foremen have in this industry when they become a foreman?

For the Intentional Change Model, use these types of questions to focus on getting someplace that honors your ideal self. You can also use this change theory—or SOP—to make yourself more competitive for the roles you want when you leave active duty. Use it for one. Use it for both. It works either way. Some examples of common learning goals for a transition include the following:

- Complete Maintenance Manager certification process

- Obtain OSHA Safety Certificate

- Translate military certifications to civilian language, using plain English to describe achievements

- Put together a resume

- Do some mock interviews

- Interview a couple shop foremen in the preferred industry

- Contact the military transition assistance person

- Put together a LinkedIn profile

- Adjust social media pages with a future role in mind (in other words, make sure you know what your future boss will be thinking when they look at your postings)

- Talk to a financial planner to better understand how savings and income requirements will support the transition

Experimentation and Practice

After you've defined and executed on your learning goals, you are ready for the final step in the Intentional Change Model—experimentation and practice. You don't become an expert overnight. Some experts have thrown out the statistic that it takes more than 10,000 hours of work to be an expert for one particular thing. Other researchers have proved that 5,000 hours might do for certain skill. The point is this: it's going to take some work.

Do you remember how long it took you to become awesome in your military career field? How long did it take for you to feel like you really mastered your military occupational specialty? You likely did the same task or series of tasks over and over countless times until you gained your level of mastery. You've done this before, and you can do it again.

Some of these new tasks or skills will challenge you immensely while some others might be a lot easier for you to do. Don't be afraid to experiment and try some new things when you're operating in this space. Keep track of what you're doing and how you feel while doing those new things. While it's true that not everything will work for you, you will likely discover that you might be really good at something you never thought you'd be good at. For example, you might find out that you enjoy working with people when you used to hate working with groups of people in your military job.

Keep in mind that you will constantly be experimenting and trying out new behaviors as you prepare to find your first civilian job—and after you start in the new role. These will be times of growth and development and change. Be prepared to make mistakes and try new approaches.

A Story of Using the Intentional Change Model

Norah was a consultant in an intense firm where she was under constant pressure to grow her revenue. After a career that lasted decades, she pivoted from working at the firm and went to work for herself.

Norah had the hardest time saying no—telling clients that she didn't want to do certain work anymore. At first, she felt like she was failing in her new business because she was declining work that she knew would generate income. Her work on "Ideal Self" served as a reminder of why she stepped away from the high-pressure environment. Her learning goals included new skills and certifications in leadership coaching. It took some time for Norah to practice and experiment with turning down lucrative work that she was really good at (but hated). In the end, Norah was able to do smaller projects for non-profits that might not have been as profitable but gave her great joy. She stuck with her core values and did something different—something that didn't bring in as much money but made her happy.

Schlossberg's Transition Model

The "one size fits all" model doesn't always work, so here's another way to look at your upcoming change—another model for your toolbox. I know what you're thinking. "Ugh, more theory? I don't want to read that stuff anymore." You don't have to read the theory stuff if you don't want to read it. It's okay. Feel free to just flip through the next couple pages.

Then again, maybe the Intentional Change Theory isn't your thing or maybe you just want to look at things a different way. Social scientists have used Schlossberg's Transition Model to help them build an understanding of the things that are involved when veterans leave active duty and move on to the civilian world. This model looks at how people see themselves compared to the rest of society.

The theory plays out all the time. The first time you or your spouse went to your commander's quarters (please start calling them houses) for a gathering, you wanted to make a good impression, so you probably spent a little bit of time thinking what you were going to wear. When you got to the event, you and your significant other undoubtedly looked around to see what everybody else was wearing so you could compare it to your choices to determine if you successfully navigated the cultural and social rules for the occasion. Was your spouse rewarded with nods of approval, or did people turn away and speak quietly when your spouse walked into the room? These social cues told you how you and your spouse were fitting in, and they were based on the concept of how others saw you.

You'll find yourself doing this more often after you leave active duty. Here are some examples of how you are likely to compare yourself to the people around you:

- "I just hit send on the e-mail. Wait, was I too short? Maybe I should've asked them about their weekend first before I demanded an update on the project. People are way more 'flowery' with their e-mails than I am with mine."

- Did you get to the meeting on time, but then you were upset because your boss or supervisor was twenty minutes late? Before you lost your temper, did you wonder if their newborn kept your boss up all night? Was there an accident on your boss's drive into work?

It's important to see yourself by looking at yourself through somebody else's eyes. How do they see me? As you leave active duty and PCS into the civilian world, you will have to start modifying your assumptions to better match what civilians are doing. The two examples above—sending e-mails and not losing your mind when meetings don't start on time—are just the beginning. (Seriously, meetings rarely start on time and when meetings kick off ten to twenty minutes behind schedule, it turns out that the world doesn't spontaneously combust.)

There are three pieces to Schlossberg's Transition Model: moving in, moving through, and moving out. Each of these stages requires you, as the moving party, to continually compare what you're doing and thinking to what other people around you are doing and thinking. Comparing the "doing" is pretty easy because you can look around and see that your office attire is good-to-go. You can read your report and somebody else's report and see how you measure up. The "thinking" analysis is a little trickier. It requires your attention to all the social cues that people are giving you as you move through the transition process.

Moving In

In the moving in phase, everything is new. You'll be issued a new boss who uses her first name instead of a title. When you call a superior by Sir or Ma'am or Mister or Misses, you'll get funny looks. When they look at you oddly, this is your social cue to adjust your behavior and just use her first name. It'll happen.

You're going through what's called a transformative process. Earlier, we talked about how you will be changing your assumptions about a lot of things. During your military service, it is assumed that you call your superior by Sir or Ma'am if they're an officer. It's assumed that you call GS-civilians who are in positions above you as Mister or Misses. It's assumed that you will call your Master Gunnery Sergeant by his full title if you don't know him really well, and if you're calling him "Master Gunns," chances are that you've known Master Gunns for a while, and you think he's pretty cool. Your behavior has been regulated by a strict sense of rules dictated by your branch of service and even by your military specialty. All that gets thrown out the window when you leave active duty, which is why the moving in phase can be so challenging.

This is also why you'll be more likely to leave your first civilian job if you can't figure it out pretty quickly. You'll learn that civilians have different requirements when you need their help on projects. Because you're not going to walk around with your rank in your back pocket and pull it out when you need somebody to "get it done"; you will need to change your assumptions about something as simple as sending an e-mail. Here are more examples for some assumptions you might need to change in the very near future:

EVENT	CURRENT ASSUMPTION	YOUR NEW ASSUMPTION
Sending an e-mail	Short is better. No need to pay attention to spelling or use full sentences.	People will judge me on the quality of my e-mails. If I spell words wrongly and don't use sentences, people will make assumptions about my capabilities.
Attending a meeting	Meetings run with formal structure and start on time.	Each meeting is different depending on who is holding the meeting and what the meeting is about.
Holding a meeting	I'm in charge. I'll talk as long as I need to talk. If you're not five minutes early, you're late.	How I treat my coworkers determines how they'll work for me in the future. They'll call me the meeting tyrant if I run my meetings rigidly.
Choosing your attire	I pretty much wear DoD issued pajamas to work. Super-easy dress code.	People might make assumptions about my capabilities by the way I dress at work and when they see me out of work. People actually look at my shoes.
Political correctness	If I have rank on someone, I can say whatever I want as long as it's not an EO thing.	Political correctness is a thing. If I don't follow the rules, it can get me fired. "He/him, them/they" is a real thing.
Swearing at work	I can swear whenever I feel like it.	People will judge my emotional intelligence based on how often I lose my temper. If I swear, people might think I'm losing my cool.

Twenty-four-hour clock	Military time is the best thing since sliced bread. Everybody should use it.	If I use military time, people might be intimidated by this reminder that I used to be on active duty. People will be embarrassed they don't know what time I mean.
Sir/Ma'am	100% required for a senior officer.	My boss might think I'm kissing up. My boss might think I'm being sarcastic. My boss might think it's cool.
Hanging out with coworkers after work	This is where I get to blow off some steam. Time to get my drink on.	Whatever I do or say at these events can impact my career. I need to be attentive to how other people are acting.

Moving Through

As you become more comfortable with your civilian job and in your home life, you will start the moving through phase. This means you're now fully immersed in your civilian life, and you have become proficient in adjusting your old assumptions to fit in with the civilians around you. You have left behind all those acronyms you loved to hate during your active service and have started talking like a regular person again. Your military uniform has likely made it into a Zip Lock bag under your bed and your spouse has "de-militarized" a couple rooms in your house. Keep in mind that you still need to challenge assumptions during this phase by "checking yourself" when you're talking in office meetings or sending e-mails.

In this phase, you need to develop new support structures to help you at home and at work. Try connecting with a Military Affinity Group if they have one in your civilian workplace. Those groups bring veterans together so you buddy team your way through stuff at work and at home. If your employer doesn't have a Military Affinity Group, consider starting one. Chapter 10 provides all the tools you'll need to understand Military Affinity Groups.

Moving Out

As you move out, you've left the honeymoon stage of your civilian job where it may have been exciting to start something new. Sometimes you might feel like "it's just another day at the office." In this final phase of transition, you have assimilated into the civilian world and can easily walk among them. The problem is some veterans never make it this far.

The moving out phase may cause self-doubt as you fully experience the loss of all those systems of care you had on active duty. Leaving behind the structure and camaraderie can be challenging, making it hard to fully integrate. It's okay to feel like you are operating out of your comfort zone. Embrace it.

No Easy Button Answer

As you are experimenting with the new you and learning new behaviors and skills, be wary of hitting the easy button. You may have been an amazing Marine who could run the logistics office and make sure that the containers made it from the railhead to the ship to the final destination on time every time. Maybe people came to you as the expert and urgently sought your skills. Taking that logistics job with UPS or FedEx or Amazon might seem like a seamless transition because the stuff you did on active duty is an incredible match.

However, be sure to bring out your work from Chapters 3 and 4 to see if the civilian job looks like it would be a good match for your future self. Does it mesh with the values you identified? Does it fit in to your personal vision statement? These tools can arm you to make good decisions in finding a job where you'll still be working twenty-four months after your transition. That's the goal here.

3

TAKING STOCK

We all struggle with the question of personal meaning throughout our lives. At your basic training school, you didn't have a good idea of "the meaning of life" until your drill sergeants or cadre told you what it would be each day. Yet, you graduated and over time, you built on your basic skills and started to stretch your leadership skills. It took time and it wasn't easy. Throughout your career, you've been under constant scrutiny by your leaders. They told you what to do—or what not to do—to get promoted or learn new skills. You followed these directions and developed into who you are as a Soldier, Seaman, Marine, Airman—a leader. Now, it's time to take stock and determine how that will influence where you go as a civilian employee.

This process can be challenging but taking time to determine how you really want to live is healthy and necessary. Without this step of taking stock, you could end up jumping from role to role—or maybe even town to town—searching for your place in the civilian world.

Let's start by finding the people who have provided support and inspiration in your life. Identifying specific moments where you felt supported or inspired should leave you feeling positive and hopeful. When you put yourself in this state, your body may experience a biological shift that makes you feel more relaxed. Your breathing will become more comfortable, and your creativity may be released. All this will help you be more open to new information and self-discovery.

Who Helped You

Think about the people who have helped you the most in life. As you consider which names to write, say to yourself, "Without this person, I would not have accomplished what I have, or be the person that I am today." You have heard these stories many times during the countless promotion ceremonies you've attended. Now it's time to create your own list. Complete the chart below with your thoughts on these experiences.

NAME	WHAT DID THIS PERSON DO OR SAY?	WHAT DID YOU LEARN FROM THIS MOMENT?

Continue reflecting on these situations and the results until you feel ready to explore your dreams for this next phase of your life, and to imagine your future self. For this work to be successful, you need to be genuinely excited about who you could become.

Values that Guide your Life

Your values are created through a unique combination of your life experiences, relationships, and your personality. Values and beliefs can change over time—particularly after large events—so now is the time to review your values. By taking the time to reflect, you can make more deliberate decisions about what path to take in this next phase of your life.

The next pages have a list of words that may speak to you and help you identify the things that are most important to you.

1. Start by reviewing this list and circling anything that feels important to you or any word that jumps off the page.

2. Feel free to fill in any words that come to mind that aren't on this list. There are blank spots at the bottom of the page for your own thoughts.

You might find yourself thinking, "I should value this, so I'm going to circle it." Think hard and choose based on your true feelings, not what you "'should" feel or do. Remember, no one will see your choices unless you choose to share them so be honest with yourself about what's truly important.

In Part Two of the exercise, you will be narrowing down your first pass into the top choices. There are many ways to do this but here are a few things to consider:

- Imagine how you would feel if you were forced to give up believing in a particular value. Could you live like that?

- Think about how you would feel if your life really revolved around one of the selected values. How would this make you feel?

- Look at two values at a time, asking yourself which one of the two is more important. Drop the one that is least important.

Part One: Circle Words from This List of Values

Invention	Affection	Help	Connections	Energy
Passion	Inform	Integration	Acquisitions	Persevere
Teach	Joy	Order	Humility	Amusement
Prosperity	Mastery	Pride	Balance	Tenderness
Change	Support	Diversity	Professionalism	Seek
Wellness	Coupled	Sensitive	Spiritual	Cohesion
Enjoyment	Ingenuity	Beauty	Devotion	Family
Inquisitive	Radiance	Direct	Security	Inspire
Bravery	Forgiveness	Wealth	Instruct	Build
Distinguish	Fun	Innovation	Calm	Drama
Gamble	Knowledge	Capable	Prepare	Glamour
Abundance	Career	Educate	Thoughtful	Laughter
Teamwork	Elegance	Satisfied	Learning	Comfort
Entrepreneurial	Arousal	Love	Community	Encourage
Gratitude	Magnificence	Compassion	Attain	Greatest
Power	Commonality	Provide	Guide	Minister
Goodness	Effectiveness	Fame	Model	Fitness
Responsive	Health	Moving	Awakened	Accomplished
Holy	Adventure	Contentment	Enjoyment	Harmony
Open	Control	Enlighten	Honor	Orchestrate
Courage	Self-Respect	Spark	Originality	Danger

Entertain	Imagination	Outdo	Home	Excellence
Impact	Patience	Dedicated	Exhilaration	Improve
Peace	Delight	Experiment	Toughness	People
Dependable	Expert	Influence	Nurturing	Design
Endurance	Awe	Perfect	Speed	Rules
Stimulate	Generosity	Persuade	Grace	Friendship
Accepting	Plan	Score	Superiority	United
Competition	Foster	Attentive	Winning	Playful
Kindness	Synthesize	Success	Pleasure	Assist
Coach	Transform	Dream	Loyalty	Artistic
Triumph	Prevail	Strength	Charisma	Trustworthy
Serenity	Sensual	Govern	Truth	Quest
Purpose	Thrill	Honesty	Bliss	Service
Understand	Uncover	Respect	Standards	Empathy
Appreciation	Refined	Intimacy	Create	Unique
God	Sincerity	Discover	Uplifting	Space
Advancement	Experience	Integrity	Religious	Humor
Vulnerable	Venture	Justice	Speculate	Renewal
Risk	Responsible	Structure	Tolerance	Freedom
Sports	Spontaneous	Leadership	Attraction	Romance

_____ _____ _____ _____ _____

_____ _____ _____ _____ _____

Part Two: Find Your Most Important Values

Now that you've chosen all the words that speak to you, narrow your list to ten. Review each circled word and put a check mark next to the ones that feel really important. If you get stuck, look at the pointers from the beginning of this section. Look at all your checked words and list the top ten here.

1.   6.

2.   7.

3.   8.

4.   9.

5.   10.

Look over this list carefully. How do you feel when you read these words? Do they seem to represent a deep part of you? Does your list contain words that reflect who you are right now, or who you want to be? Do you feel hope or excitement as you look at this list?

Part Three: Rank Your Top Five Values

Now it's time to narrow the list even further and rank them. Look over your list of ten and choose the five words that are really the most important. You may feel uncomfortable giving up any of the values on your top ten list. Remember, your values may change over time. Try to find the words that really show how you want your life to look from this point forward.

As you write down the top five, rank the list with #1 as your most important to #5 being the least important. Try to define each word.

1.
2.
3.
4.
5.

Part Four: Reflect on Your Results

This may have been a lot of work for you. Maybe you've never taken time to think about what is most important to you. Or maybe it took energy to move your thinking from what you valued in your military life to what you want your life to look like now. Keep going with this process. The work that you put in now will ease your transition and help you reach a place of contentment quicker. Here are some questions that will help you figure out what to do with the results of this values exercise.

- How would you feel if your post-military life had all five of the values in it?

- What kinds of jobs or activities could be in your life that would help fulfill your top five values?

- Does anything need to change in your life to make room for the most important values?

- What would your life look like if you only had one or two of your top five values in your civilian job?

Personal SWOT Analysis

SWOT stands for Strengths, Weaknesses, Opportunities, and Threats. The SWOT analysis was invented in the 1960s to help businesses organize their thoughts on strategy and how to move the organization forward. It is still used today in mostly the same format as it was when it was originally introduced.

The SWOT analysis is not just for business, however. It a useful development exercise that can help you evaluate your direction and personal goals. You can use this questionnaire to do a SWOT analysis on yourself as you continue your preparations on transitioning from the military.

If you're struggling to find weaknesses or strengths, try reviewing your last two or three performance evaluations.

Be aware that personal bias will creep into your answers when completing your personal SWOT analysis. Backing up your lists with examples or asking one or two people to give you feedback are great ways to help minimize bias and create a more valuable tool.

STRENGTHS	WEAKNESSES
List everything at which you excel. Include skills, certifications, achievements, and personal qualities.	List areas in your life that need improvement. Consider any skills that you will need to obtain to succeed in this next phase.

OPPORTUNITIES	THREATS
What things have happened or could happen that would help you succeed in the civilian world?	Is there anything that is holding you back from success? What could disrupt your path?

Once you finish the grid, you can use this information to create a plan. Look at each box individually, and compare the information across the rows and columns. What can you learn from all this? Here are some things to consider as you use this information to create a personal vision statement.

- **Align your next steps with your strengths**. Evaluate potential opportunities through the lens of your personal strengths. If you have the chance to pursue something that is well-suited to your strengths, be sure to explore the opportunity with eagerness.

- **Examine any threats to your opportunities**. It's important to remember that not all decisions are under your control. Take a closer look at any threats that you listed and consider how they could play into the opportunities. Opportunities with few or no threats are the easiest to pursue but taking the easy path might not be the right one for you. Develop plans on how to minimize threats to your opportunities so you know how to react when they show up.

- **Use your strengths to address weaknesses**. Looking at your weaknesses, do you see anything that could directly interfere with your ability to pursue an opportunity? If not, that's excellent! But you might have a couple weaknesses that need some work before you're ready to pursue your dreams. Look for ways that you can use your strengths to overcome them or make a plan to eliminate those weaknesses that will get in the way.

Personal Vision Paragraph

There are many other ways to do self-reflection and you should take the time to use any tools that work for you. Some other options include the following:

- Create a bucket list.

- List your favorite things to do at work and outside of work.

- Determine if there's anything you are doing in your life that you don't like.

- Set a timer for two minutes and write down whatever comes first to your mind and follow that path for the writing exercise.

- Describe a scenario, person, or place that inspires you.

- Reflect on what you would do if you just won the lottery and received $50M. How would your life and work look?

- Picture yourself ten years from now and write down what kind of work you are doing, who is important in your life, what possessions do you treasure, and how you spend your free time.

Once you have explored your thoughts and feelings, it's time to write a paragraph that explains your desired future. This vision for your desired life will serve as your starting point for a learning plan. Start with how you want things to look five years from now.

Although the paragraph can take many forms, we recommend that you begin with a brief statement of what you want in your future. Then, expand your thoughts. Once you write one paragraph that reflects "Your Personal Vision," you can extend the vision for as long as you wish—ten years or twenty years from now—using other paragraphs. Use your reflections from this guide to cover your ideal life and work. Be sure to cover your work, friends and family, your health, community, and spiritual life.

Keep in mind that the whole point of this exercise is to help you find a life that is compatible with who you are now, and who you want to be over the next five to twenty-five years. Try not to rush this exercise.

MY PERSONAL VISION

Learning Goal Sheet

Let's take the next step in taking stock and achieving your Personal Vision. As you examine all the work that you've completed so far, what stands out in your current strengths that can be used to move toward your Personal Vision? Are there gaps between who you are now and who you want to be or how you want to live your life? What changes do you think you'll need to make to achieve your vision? These are the items that need to be covered in your Learning Goals. This book has space for two goals, but you can list more. It's probably good to list between one and four goals so you don't get overwhelmed with the process.

What are "Learning Goals"?

You have a great deal of experience setting goals that require you to perform and deliver a certain result. These are called performance or outcome goals and they aren't always effective when it comes to living out your personal vision. Instead, this book focuses on setting goals for learning. Learning is defined as "the acquisition of knowledge or skills through experience, study, or by being taught." In other words, what do you need to know, or be able to do, to live the life you want?

Learning Goal Sheet Example 1

To help you create two Learning Goals, let's look at an example for a logistics officer who is leaving the military after twelve years of service. The Values Exercise revealed that her top five values are: Structure, Connections, Dedicated, Create, and Wellness. In her personal vision statement, she discusses how she wants to help a civilian organization deliver better service. She would love to create a new operations mindset for a struggling company. Upon reflection, she realizes that she wants a role with leadership responsibilities and to have the quickest impact, she has decided that focusing on small businesses makes the most sense. It could also support her desire to make connections because she will be working with a tight-knit group.

She also realizes that civilian businesses (even non-profit organizations) place a significant amount of emphasis on profits and losses, which is not something she was used to addressing in her prior logistical work with the Department of Defense. To make this happen, she knows she needs to learn more about how small businesses measure profits and losses so she can talk about what financial results her new company can expect.

Here is what her first learning goal sheet might look like:

LEARNING GOAL (WHAT DO YOU NEED TO KNOW, OR BE ABLE TO DO?) *Understand traditional company profit and loss measurements*	First action step	When will you do this?	Who will help you?
	Take online Small Business Financials course	May–June	Son will participate in course so we can have discussions about content
	Second action step	When will you do this?	Who will help you?
	Meet with two to four small business owners to understand operations challenges in their world.	Summer	Local small business association can help make these introductions
	Third action step	When will you do this?	Who will help you?
	Attend Chamber of Commerce small business roundtable meeting as guest	Next meeting is October 4	Neighbor is VP of local Chamber of Commerce Board

Learning Goal Sheet Example 2

The next example highlights the thought process of an Artilleryman who is leaving the military after six years of service. The Values Exercise revealed that his top five values are: Security, Provide, Expert, Responsive, and Freedom. In his personal SWOT analysis, he identified one of his strengths as planning capabilities, particularly developing threat environment plans. The analysis also pointed out that he is concerned about the "threat" of financial pressure limiting him from working in a role he really enjoys—rather than just taking a job that can pay the bills. He knows he is going to have to prepare himself well in advance of his exit to make sure he can live his values.

Putting the pieces together from his Taking Stock exercises, he begins to see that a career in safety coordination appeals to him. Some of the skills he learned in his Advance Leadership courses will help this. He just needs to figure out how to translate those into civilian language. Plus, he's going to have to learn a few things about how safety protocols work in the civilian world. This is an example of how one of his Learning Goal sheets might look:

LEARNING GOAL (WHAT DO YOU NEED TO KNOW, OR BE ABLE TO DO?) *Create a resume and develop interview skills that show my qualifications for Safety Coordinator roles.*	First action step	When will you do this?	Who will help you?
	Obtain Occupational Safety Certification	Fifteen months starting in January	Spouse will help me to enroll and discuss how to make time for this in our lives.
	Second action step	**When will you do this?**	**Who will help you?**
	Meet with expert consultant on how to improve my resume (for example, military search firm).	Summer	Friend who left the military last year can connect me with the company he used.
	Third action step	**When will you do this?**	**Who will help you?**
	Practice interviewing to ensure I can explain how my military experience applies.	October to December	Niece's husband does HR recruiting and could help find someone to do practice interviews.

Your Learning-Goal Sheet

Now it's your turn. What do you need to know—or what do you need to be able to do—to take the next step and pursue your dreams in the next phase of your life? You should create between two and four learning goals using this template.

LEARNING GOAL 1 (WHAT DO YOU NEED TO KNOW, OR BE ABLE TO DO?)	First action step	When will you do this?	Who will help you?
	Second action step	When will you do this?	Who will help you?
	Third action step	When will you do this?	Who will help you?

LEARNING GOAL 2 (WHAT DO YOU NEED TO KNOW, OR BE ABLE TO DO?)	First action step	When will you do this?	Who will help you?
	Second action step	When will you do this?	Who will help you?
	Third action step	When will you do this?	Who will help you?

4

BUILDING SUPPORT SYSTEMS

While you were creating your learning goals, you noticed that you needed to complete a section on "who will help you" for each action step. That's because you have all these choices and decisions to make, and you need people surrounding you, who will help you talk through your ideas, make connections for you, or just keep you on track to the timeline you set.

It's important to acknowledge—both to you and others—that transitioning out of the military is a big change. We know that when change happens, we may feel alone with our feelings or experiences. If you are the "first" of your peers to leave, these feelings might be more intense. That's why support is essential during this time. Find and lean on people who you know you can trust. Be open and clear about what you need and learn to depend on them for advice or comfort.

If you feel like you need more help than what your friends and family can provide during this time, consider reaching out for professional help. One-on-one therapy sessions can provide a safe space to share your true thoughts and feelings. You don't have to worry about "having it together" or "appearing tough." Just show up and be honest about what's going on.

Personal Board of Directors

A Personal Board of Directors is one way to create a go-to support system as you navigate this transition. It's a small group of people that you go to for support and advice. Their main role is to provide feedback on your decisions, opportunities, and challenges. And if you choose the right members, you'll get unfiltered feedback that you can't always get from your closest circle. Your Personal Board of Directors does not usually meet as a whole group, but it's possible that a week won't go by without you consulting someone from the group.

By carefully selecting these people in your life, you can create a group that has a strong interest in seeing you succeed and thrive. The board normally consists of five to eight people that you can rely on to act as your personal sounding board as you work through this transition. If you want to create the smoothest, most successful transition, you must tap into the broadest possible base of people who are more seasoned than you are and can view your choices objectively. You want these various viewpoints to provide mirrors that bring you clarity when they are all put together.

How Can a Board Help You?

- **Make Connections for You.** Each person on your Board knows people you don't know, and they have experiences you've never had. They can be your connection to key contacts in the civilian world, which can help you. They can sell your skills and experience to hiring managers on the lookout for talent. They can arrange key meetings or trainings that help you meet your goals. They might truly be the key to a door that would normally be closed for you.

- **Challenge You.** Every Board member will not share your views. You want it that way. The very best members will actively challenge you and ask the really hard questions about your plans and decisions. This will help you get clear on anything you might be missing.

- **Provide Support**. You might expect your personal board of directors to help you in hard times, but they will also be there to celebrate your success. Make sure you share both good times and bad times with these people to create the most meaningful relationships.

- **Introduce New Experiences**: You can learn so much from just observing these experienced people navigate their civilian work challenges, and even their personal lives. They will know networking groups, training opportunities, and support systems that you would not have been exposed to in your military life. Ask questions and join them in as many experiences as possible.

- **Hold You Accountable**. Even though it's last on this list, it might be the most important role of the members of your Personal Board of Directors. Each person can hold you accountable for your actions and behavior impacting your success. You should make sure they understand the importance of this role and share your detailed plans so they can ask questions about your progress.

Assembling Your Personal Board of Directors

The key to creating the best Personal Board of Directors is identifying a diverse group of individuals that have a rich mix of experiences. As you start to consider names, think about asking and approaching people who:

- Genuinely care about you as a person and your success

- Hold a position you would like to have someday

- Are experts in an area you need to learn more about

- Have worked in the civilian world their entire careers so you can gain an entirely new perspective

- Have transitioned from the military into the civilian world and thus can relate to your exact experience

- Are skilled at looking at a company or industry to explain how it's working now and what trends you'll be seeing

- Can provide sincere encouragement so you can invest in yourself and your development

- Can be completely honest with you and not worry about upsetting you

Step One: Map out Your Current Supporters

Fill out the chart below. Think about who is already providing support or advice to you. Put their names in the boxes below and then list their role in your life based on the definitions that are provided. In the third column, get clear on what you want from these individuals. What specific advice or help do you want from them?

In Step Two, you are going to take a closer look at this current list and decide if the group is diverse enough. You'll then go back to this chart to determine if the current members should stay or go based on what you need.

NAME	ROLE	PURPOSE	STAY OR GO

ROLE	DEFINITION
Mentor	Senior person who can share experience
Peer	Trusted colleague who can be honest with you
Expert	Knowledgeable individual who can teach you new things
Coach	Someone who can ask you tough questions
Friend	Personal relationship that provides emotional support

Step Two: Diversify Your Board

Strive for diversity in background, education, geography, expertise, and personal situation. Who or what is missing that you believe would help you along the way? Are all the same gender and from the same geography? Are they all from the same generation? Everyone can benefit from the perspectives of someone older and younger than them. Do you have too many friends and not enough experts or mentors? What specific areas of expertise will you need to tap into based on your Personal Vision? What mentors will you need to make the right connections to help you through this transition? With more perspectives, you can create a fuller picture.

NEW BOARD MEMBER	ROLE	PURPOSE

Keep in mind that you'll want to choose Board members who actually interest you. Having this genuine interest in your selected people will make it easier to develop and maintain the relationship, and it can prevent things from feeling strictly transactional.

Step Three: Create Your Final List

Now it's time to go back and refine your list of who should "sit" on your Personal Board of Directors. Look at your work from Step One. Rewrite any of the names that have a Yes in the Stay column. Then, pull the names from Step Two in which you made deliberate decisions on diversifying your Board. Once you've completed the chart below, be sure to take one more look to ensure nothing is missing. You might even consider coming back to the list in a day or two after you've had a chance to step away from the exercise and let your thoughts settle.

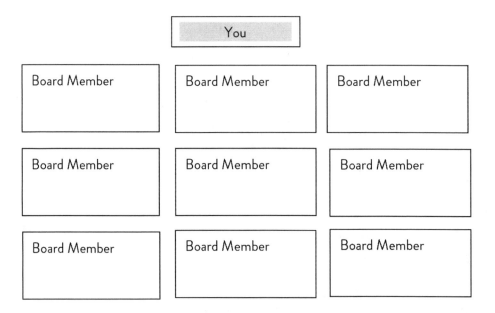

Step Four: Regularly Evaluate Your Board

Your Personal Board of Directors is not a static group. Continually take stock of who is on your board, and whether they are really serving the role you need. Most importantly, assess your needs regularly and determine who else might need to be there. Even when you get through the initial transition, you should keep a Personal Board of Directors to guide you through each stage of your career and your life. It's always good to have a group of people that you trust surrounding you with advice, support, and connections.

Communicating with Your Personal Board of Directors

Warm contacts are always easier than "cold calls." If you already have a good relationship with someone who made your Personal Board of Directors, you can reach out with an e-mail updating them on your plans for leaving the military and asking if they'd be open to meeting for coffee or scheduling a phone call to discuss some of your thoughts.

If you are looking to connect with people you don't know well, ask friends or family to introduce you to potential Board members. Using LinkedIn can help you find possible Board members, and you can ask your common connections for an introduction. Finally, if you picked out someone with no clear personal connection, look for shared experiences that would make it easier to reach out. Obviously, if he or she has a military background, that's an easy one, but maybe there's a love of a particular sports team, or an interest in books that could make the initial conversation easier. If you're struggling on building your board, don't fret. Try joining and participating in a veterans group like the American Legion or Veterans of Foreign Wars. Non-profit veteran organizations are filled with people just like you and you'll never know who may want to join your board to help out.

You'll be surprised how many people will be willing to help you work through this transition. In general, people like to help, and most people will be flattered that you asked them to be on your Personal Board of

Directors. You may get some rejections and sometimes you won't hear back at all, but you don't need a yes from every person you ask. Keep in mind that you are also a valuable connection for your Board members, even if that seems difficult to see as you're just beginning your civilian life. You never know when you'll be able to return the favor and help out one of your Board members.

You might cross paths with some of your Board members naturally—if they are family members or close friends for example. If not, reach out to them every so often. E-mail or call just to invite them to lunch to catch up. Be sure to keep track of their interests or projects so you can ask them about what they've been doing. Then, you can share things about your own progress. It's important to work on building the relationship so you aren't just contacting them when you urgently need help. The exact frequency will depend on many things, but it's reasonable to get in touch around four times a year.

5

LEARNING THE LANGUAGE

When you first joined the military, there was a lot that you didn't know. You witnessed new recruits referring to senior NCOs as "Sir" and then get reprimanded for it. You didn't know what to do with the ends of your boot laces. ("Do I tuck them in? Let them hang? Wrap them around the top of my boots a couple times?") You understood military time by doing simple math and adding a twelve to anything that came up after noon. After some time, you pretty much just knew that it gets dark around 2100 and that you needed to be in formation by 0630. And you figured out what to do with those boot laces. Learning made it possible for you to assimilate into the military culture which made it easier for you to get to chow, get your work done and maybe even get promoted a couple times.

Your initial training helped quite a bit in helping you "become" a service member. You spend months with seasoned experts to learn the skills and a new language. When you finished basic and advanced training, you could march and salute. You could qualify with your primary weapon, and you learned the basics of how to do your new military occupational skills. The DoD really, really wanted you to join and be ready. The DoD doesn't really, really want you to leave though. It's not going to spend the same amount of money to prepare you to leave, nor is it going to give you the same level of training to prepare you for your new, civilian occupational skills (COS).

Wouldn't it be great if your commanding officer would give you six to ten months to work full time to get ready for your transition? You could spend a couple weeks putting your new wardrobe together and doing mock-interviews. You could brush up on all the new trends in whatever field you choose and spend weeks working with those new job skills and applying them to the new work trends and becoming proficient in your new COS. But it doesn't work that way. This part is going to be on you.

The Cost of Preparing You

The Army's Training and Doctrine Command estimates that it costs between $22,000 and $40,000 to recruit an Army soldier and get them to enlist. The Army will then spend close to $200,000 for each soldier to get them through basic training and their Advanced Initial Training (AIT). So, for each soldier, the DoD spends between $220,000 and $240,000 just to get them through their primary military occupational specialty training course.

Plus, the DoD needs to enlist an estimated 80,000 to 90,000 each and every year because 3% to 12% will not make it through the basic course and advanced training. The grand total: 17.6 billion dollars each year. Getting you into a uniform and making sure you adopt the military culture requires money, and just as importantly, it didn't happen overnight. Keep in mind that they won't spend anywhere near this amount of money to get you ready to leave service and get your first civilian job.

At this point, you may be thinking, "What does any of this have to do with me learning a new language?" Part of your COS training needs to focus on your ability to receive information from civilians, understand it, and transmit information back to them in a way that everybody understands. Unfortunately, it's not as easy as it sounds. You can't just start thinking and acting and talking like a civilian because you used to be one before you joined the military. Remember, you spent countless hours and months of your time (and lost quite a bit of sleep), learning everything you needed to know so you could do a satisfactory job once you got to your first unit. These things take time and effort, and you need to put in some time to get ready for your transition. You've started the work if you've completed the exercises in the previous chapters. You have a better understanding of why you joined in the first place, who you are now, and what kind of person you might be when you're not wearing combat boots to work. Keep those lessons with you as you work on each step in the process.

It Starts with First Contact

Your new bosses and coworkers won't have your level of awareness of what you learned and what you accomplished during your military service. Research shows that while civilian businesses are actively pursuing you as a veteran, they don't really understand what they are getting. Human resource leaders say things like, "We don't know the language, and the structure of the military organization. When I'm in these interviews, I always have to ask multiple follow-up questions just so I can understand what they're trying to explain."

That could be you in the interview if you don't work on learning the language. You've served in uniform for years. You worked hard and learned incredible skills. You became an expert at something—a "no kidding" expert. And you flubbed an interview because you weren't able to tell your interviewer in basic terms what you did for a living. You need to be able to talk the talk to be competitive.

Language is a significant part of culture and culture is the #1 reason that you'll stay in your first job for longer than twenty-four months. This chapter will help you better understand how you interact with other people in the workplace. In the chapters ahead, there's additional information about emotional intelligence, and the role it will play in your ability to mesh with your new coworkers. But for now, focus on learning the lingo and what civilians consider acceptable conduct in the workplace.

Ass Chewing

Ass chewing. Wire brushing. Dressing someone down. You've seen it happen. Some poor Major forgot to update his slides before the big briefing and got called out during the briefing in front of his peers. Or maybe a lead recruiter "rolled a goose egg" for three months in a row and was lambasted during the biweekly staff meeting by his Sergeant Major. The words were something like, "You're absolutely worthless. Seriously! You're nothing more than a hood ornament for this organization. How am I supposed to make my recruiting numbers if you can't even put one Soldier on the board every month? Dude, you had one job and that's to enlist X soldiers a month. You're a worthless piece of shit." While it's nice to imagine that the lambasting you just read was made up, it wasn't. Conversations like this happen all the time in the military world. As a result, the subject of the ass chewing simply retired. And that interaction played a significant role in his decision to leave active duty. There were no consequences for the Sergeant Major.

What would happen to a civilian leader if something like this happened in a civilian workplace? In the most extreme cases, the injured party would file a union grievance or a lawsuit. The senior leaders in the organization would likely initiate an internal investigation which might mean hiring a third-party investigator. Once the investigation is over, the ass-chewer would be terminated, assuming they were still with the organization. Situations like this are distracting and expensive for employers to handle and as a result, it's a rare thing for a civilian employer to tolerate abusive conduct from managers or even other coworkers.

Post-Traumatic Stress

Keep in mind that civilian employers are less likely to understand that a service member's misconduct or bad temper in the workplace may be a byproduct of Post-Traumatic Stress (PTS). The Department of Defense's National Center for PTS reports that veterans of Operation Iraqi Freedom (OIF) and

Operation Enduring Freedom (OEF) have PTSD rates ranging from 12% to 20%. This could be something that you are encountering in your personal life. Maybe you know you suffer from PTS related issues and are seeking help. Maybe you know you suffer from PTS issues and are pretending you don't have a problem. Maybe you don't have PTSD. Any way you look at it, your ability to calmly and rationally engage with your managers and coworkers will play a key role in whether you stay, leave, or get fired.

If you think you have an anger issue or if your spouse says that you might have a problem, deal with it. Deal with it right now and start talking to someone. If you're still on active duty, talk to your military physician and make sure it's documented in your medical file. Depending on the severity of your condition, you may even be entitled to a VA disability rating.

There are countless organizations within the DoD framework, and in the nonprofit space that are there to help you with your PTSD. Spend a little time on the internet and see what might work best for you.

Profanity

While today's civilian workplace is more relaxed compared to twenty years ago, using profanity during work can still carry some social stigma. A human resource (HR) leader for a hospital in the Midwest encountered a former military employee in the workplace who used profanity all the time. He had no regard for anyone that heard his remarks. The HR leader met with the veteran to explain that it wasn't appropriate to swear in front of hospital employees or patients, even when he was "really upset." The employee in this case was lucky because the HR leader knew he was a veteran and was willing to take time to discuss the rules of the road. The HR leader remarked, "I was amazed that he could be walking around the hospital talking like he was on active duty without ever knowing he needed to change his behavior. The cultures just aren't the same."

According to the Society for Human Resources Management, there are three factors you can assess to see if the language you use in the workplace is appropriate: (1) who is using the profanity, (2) what words are used, and (3) what is the overall context of the discussion. Who does most of the swearing? Studies show that most of the people who swear are in entry-level or low-paying jobs. The higher up the ladder you climb, the less civilians swear. Generally speaking, if a manager or senior leader is swearing in the workplace, employees usually feel a little more comfortable to engage in similar conduct using the same kind of words. But you can't escalate. If the boss says "damn it" during a meeting when she's upset that a project isn't going to be delivered on time, that doesn't mean you can drop an F-bomb or amp things up like you did on active duty.

Words matter. They really do. Believe it or not, there are different tiers of swearing and you never want to be the coworker who escalates the level of language that's being used. You never want to be the first one who jumps in the water without making sure there's nothing lurking underneath. Take some time when you first start working and listen to your environment.

Most workplace swearing takes in place in the break-room and out of sight of customers or patrons. There's a reason for this. Your civilian employer will likely have spent considerable time and money to build their reputation with the public. Your employer wants you to represent the organization and its values. How are you representing the organization if you start cursing with a client or ripping off lines from your favorite cop show? Swearing in front of a customer or client is never advisable—even if the patrons are swearing.

One last thing about using profanity in the workplace: context is everything. Saying "damn it" or "shit" in a meeting is completely different than saying "damn you." Someone saying "damn you" is pretty personal and that could lead to a disciplinary issue. And never ever swear during a job interview. The interview is your first chance to make an impression, and you'll sour the whole experience because you said something that you'll regret.

Terms of Violence

When Jacob earned an in-residence seat for his advanced leadership course instead of having to do the entire class online, he told his buddies that winning his seat was like "winning a knife fight in a darkly lit room." Jacob was a Marine, and Marines talk like that sometimes. Maybe you do too. As a veteran or soon-to-be veteran, regardless of your specialty, you were engaged in the business of bringing harm or death to others. The military is in the business of lethality.

The requirement for lethality is programmed during basic training and OCS. The core component is being able to go to war and win. Nobody is going to win a war if they go into it with the mentality of "maybe nobody's going to get hurt." But the civilian world is a whole lot different—you can't talk about violence or threats of violence in a civilian workplace. You don't need to tell them winning the new account was like winning a knife fight. Just tell them you landed the new account.

At some point, it's likely one of your coworkers or maybe even your supervisor will ask you if you ever killed anyone. There isn't any right or wrong answer in this situation, but again it all comes down to context. Are they asking the question because they're simply curious? Or are they asking the question because they're worried you might be a threat to others in the office? You're never going to know why they're asking, so it's best to be prepared for the question before it comes up. If you have been in a situation where you've had to take another life, you may want to say something like: "My deployment was a long time ago and it's not something I really like talking about. But I learned a lot about myself and my ability to handle some pretty challenging situations." They'll understand what you're really saying and will probably move the conversation to another subject.

"Military Mode"

Mark was a helicopter pilot and spent fifteen years flying CONUS and led Marines during several combat tours in OIF and OEF. He left active duty with a medical pension and had several jobs before he landed a position as a project supervisor for a non-profit organization. The non-profit had a couple different offices in his home state, and Mark managed several people in his office and in satellite offices that were over a two-hour drive away. Mark was an amazing pilot and leader and teammate, but he struggled in being able to supervise civilians after he first left active duty.

"I would get upset with them because I would ask my employees to do something, and when I would check back with them later in the week, I'd find out that they hadn't done what I asked them to do, and it was endlessly frustrating," Mark remarked about trying to motivate different members of his team. Mark continued: "I would hear from other managers and coworkers they were upset at me because I would fire off an e-mail on a Monday and ask them where they were on their projects and didn't ask them about what they did over the weekend or how their kids were doing. I was stuck in military mode."

When he was on active duty, he was the master of the follow-up. He would receive his mission, issue orders to his fellow pilots and maintenance crew, and then he'd check back in with them well before any deadlines to make sure his people were doing what they were supposed to do. Military mode worked well. But those same techniques that made him an amazing combat pilot were failing him in his new civilian job. Why was this happening to him now? He was failing as a civilian leader because his communication skills weren't translating. Eventually, Mark recovered and spent a lot more time crafting what he called "softer and gentler" e-mails. Mark said, "Before I would type the e-mail, I would think to myself, 'What do I really know about this person and how can I use that knowledge to make me a better leader?'"

It took some time adjusting, but eventually Mark made time to get to know what his employees liked to do when they weren't at work, and what types of training techniques and communications worked best for them. When Mark decided he needed to communicate more "softly and gently," it really meant that he was struggling in being able to connect with his employees and needed to spend some time developing his interpersonal relationships with them.

Sir/Ma'am

You've spent years (or decades) using the military system to your advantage and playing within the social rules that were tailored for your military service. For example, when a senior officer walked into the room, someone probably called the room to attention and you all stood up and waited for the commander to instruct you to continue working "as you were."

Rank had its privileges and required respect, regardless of your feelings about that senior leader as a person. You still did the "Sir" or "Ma'am" thing and also made sure you said good morning to the Master Chief especially if you knew he hadn't had his coffee yet. The respect thing was easy in the military world, and there were surely times when things got a little comical.

At the Naval Academy in Annapolis, Maryland, tourists asked why a Lieutenant Commander was walking through the Yard as she delicately carried a stack of files in her left hand with four fingers and then, looped her coffee cup with her left pinkie finger, as she walked with her right hand completely free. The tourists would find out that the officer would be confronted by Midshipman after Midshipman, and it was pretty much one salute after another for about 100 meters. While it was comical, it also showcased the importance of courtesy and the tradition of saluting senior officers that dates back well over 150 years.

Habits like that are hard to break. You will undoubtedly be drawn to call your boss "Sir" or "Ma'am." A problem can occur if your boss is younger than you, he or she might think you're making fun of them. If colleagues are older than you, they might be bothered because those terms are linked to age, and they don't want to be considered "old." Any way you look at it, it's unlikely that anybody in a civilian business will ever want to be called "Sir" or "Ma'am." Although it may be challenging for you, you will need to get used to calling all your employees and coworkers by their first name.

What Did You Say?

Perhaps the most significant part of learning the lingo for your new COS is taking stock in how you have been communicating with your military counterparts and with your family over the length of your military service. You have developed an incredible vocabulary that is able to quickly tell other military personnel how to do things in a way that is second nature to you. But when you "go home" on leave to meet with your parents, there have likely been times where you were asked, "What did you just say?"

During a recent national emergency, an Army O-6 Operations Chief was working a joint mission with Air Force personnel to build a quick reaction force for the U.S. Capital. In the briefing, the O-6 said: "We have 72 hours to put together a joint team of 200–300 pax. I'm thinking we can start with looking at MOSs in the eleven series and see what we've got there before we can finish our staff estimate." The Air Force folks in the room asked him what an MOS was. In the Air Force, their version of the Military Occupational Specialty (MOS) is called an Air Force Specialty Code (AFSC). In other words, if your language doesn't necessarily translate between service branches, it most certainly won't translate to the civilian world.

If you have had the fantastic opportunity to work in a joint military environment, you have already witnessed how your way of speech is based on your particular branch of service. In those environments, you quickly learned that your way of speech didn't necessarily translate to other branches within the Department of Defense structure. It most certainly did not translate to foreign military personnel that you may have worked with during your deployments. You learned to take a little more time to explain what you were trying to talk about.

In addition to the wide variety of military acronyms, you will also have challenges using military time references in the civilian workforce. It is an extremely effective way to tell time. By using the twenty-four-hour clock, you will never show up at someone's house for a dinner instead of a brunch because 0800 will never be confused with 2000. Although most public transportation systems use the twenty-four-hour clock, it's pretty unlikely that your civilian coworkers are going to be using military time. That means, if you invite someone over for dinner at 1830, they're likely to look at you with a blank stare at first. Just start using civilian time, even if you are grumbling a bit when you have to spend the extra couple minutes to type the colon and the "a.m." or the "p.m." It's what civilian organizations are used to seeing in their communications.

To help you understand the words and phrases that you use in your military world that don't translate well to the civilian workplace, this table should get you started in shaping the way you speak or write.

WHAT YOU SAY	WHAT THEY SAY
1800	6 p.m.
Roger / Roger that	Okay
AAR	End of project review
Sir/Ma'am	John/Sarah
Briefing	Meeting/staff meeting
Chow	Breakfast/lunch/dinner
HRO	Human Resources
PT/PRT	Go running/work out/hit the gym
UNSAT	That's not what I was looking for

Shit show	That didn't go well. That could've gone better.
WILCO	I can do that.
Affirm	Okay/got it
Charlie Mike	Keep it going
White Paper: Meaning a one-page summary	White Paper: Meaning a twenty-to-thirty-page report that is backed up with research
Power Point Ranger	Graphic Designer
Above my pay grade	I'm not in a position to make that decision.
Acknowledged/ACK	Thanks/Okay/Got it
Cannibalize	Use work product from somebody else
Groundhog Day	Groundhog Day
Joint Operation Planning	Cross-functional teams
Red Team	Focus group
Unass	Let's get going
AWOL	We don't know where Kevin is right now.
PCS	They moved/we moved
TDY	Business trip

COB	COB or end of business day
Boots on the ground	I need you in the office or to go on a trip.
Leave	Vacation or PTO
Quarters	My place
War Gaming	Dry run/practice
Chain of Command	Hierarchy
Commanded	Supervised or directed
Deactivated	Closed/terminated operations
Mission	Task/objectives/priorities/initiatives
RECON	Data collection/analysis
Regulations/regs	Policy/guidelines/instructions
Sensitive Information	Confidential information
Fire Team/squad/shipmates	Coworkers
Superior	Supervisor or manager
Course of Action	Plan or option
War College	Master's degree/Master's program

After looking at this list of military jargon, you may dismiss the need to change your language. However, your ability to fit in with your new coworkers and with your new supervisors is paramount in a successful transition. The research shoes that veterans leave their first civilian jobs because of culture friction—their inability to mesh with the other people in the workgroup. The words or phrases that sound perfectly fine to you now will probably not work for you in the civilian workplace.

G.I. Joe Persona

Ray was an HR professional for the Army, who retired as an O-5 with a full pension. He did a great job at his interview and landed the assistant HR leader position in a mid-sized manufacturing plant in the Midwest. On his first day in the office, a senior leader in the company called Ray into his office and said, "Ray, we don't want G.I. Joe working here. I don't want to see a bunch of crazy military stuff or hear a bunch of military jargon. It scares people. I think you'll do better at this company if you come off more as a civilian."

What happened during Ray's initial engagement with his senior leadership? He learned that "they" didn't fully understand what skills and capabilities Ray was bringing into the office. He had been through several coveted leadership schools during his military career and supervised over 100 HR professionals right before he retired. Ray's skills and experience were perfect for his new position. The only problem was that his new supervisors didn't want him to present himself as "G.I. Joe." Keep in mind that his senior leader's comments weren't necessarily discriminatory. The comments showed that the senior leader understood the company culture and wanted to give Ray the upper hand by helping him synch into the new culture starting from his first day on the job. He couldn't have done that if Ray came into work and started giving orders to his subordinates and using acronyms that nobody would understand.

To fit in with his company's culture, Ray spent a considerable amount of time working on his interpersonal communication skills. He de-militarized his speech and stopped using jargon to help him fit in. He excelled in his civilian role. What you choose to do with this recommendation (to de-militarize) your speech is completely up to you. Just keep in mind that you only have one chance to give your supervisors and your coworkers a great first impression.

Attire/clothing

It's been easy for you to get ready for military work. Your boots needed to be cleaned (or polished) and then you simply grabbed a uniform out of your closet. The supply sergeant or your Exchange provided everything else you needed to dress appropriately in your military work environment.

As you're getting ready to leave active duty, it's a good time to start refreshing your wardrobe. You won't be able to do this by heading to the Exchange to buy work or casual clothes. Keep in mind that you'll be dropping into a workplace where your counterparts have already been working there for quite some time which provides opportunities to learn what was appropriate to wear for an interview, at work, and even during social engagements after work. Like the words you use, your choice of clothes will say something about you in every situation.

A Word about Quality

Your military fatigues likely lasted several years, were washed hundreds of times, and still looked great. Fatigues are made from incredibly sturdy fabric that was tested to make sure it would have the longevity that your branch of service needed to have for a daily-wear uniform.

Quality costs money

Don't be surprised when a good pair of shoes costs over $200. Your selection of shoes will say a lot about where you've been and where you're going, so don't skimp on them. Cheap clothes might look fine after a washing or two, but they'll never make it twelve months. Look for quality-built items.

Each branch of service offers an out-processing course that is designed to help you ease into civilian life. In some of those programs, you will have access to a tailor or clothing specialist who can give you some pointers on the trends in the clothing world and how that should influence the clothes you're going to buy.

There are several services that can help you put together a new wardrobe. Some services are 100% online and will pair you with a designer who will interview you to see what type of body you have, where you live, and what kind of work you want to do. Then they'll make recommendations to you, put together a box of clothing options and ship it to you. All you have to do is try it on, keep what fits, and ship the rest back. You can cancel their services any time, or you could have them send you a new box of clothes every couple weeks or months.

6

ESTABLISHING
WORK–LIFE BALANCE

You've learned that cultural friction is the main reason that service members leave their civilian jobs. Work–life balance is the runner-up to cultural friction, and it's the second leading factor that will cause you to leave your first civilian job.

Explaining Work–Life Balance

Work–life balance is defined as an individual's prioritization of work, social aspirations, and family obligations. When your work–life balance is harmonious, you are able to spend time doing the things that you want to do. The factors that go into someone's work–life balance are different for everyone. Self-development and internal growth may be important for one person, but may play less of a role for someone else. Everybody's different and the results of your Values Exercise will give you important insight to where your balance might need to be.

You should expect the factors that you used to build your work–life balance when you were on active duty will evolve as you transition to your new civilian world. Spending time with family may be a larger priority for you now that you're leaving active duty—maybe you want to catch up on some things you missed out on due to your prior work pressures, deployments, and other time you were away from home. Or maybe you want to spend more time on education where you can finish that degree you started or earn a master's degree.

When you defined your values in Chapter 3, you identified at least five things that were important to you. If you move your life away from those core values, things become a little more challenging because you aren't paying attention to the areas that really matter to you. The closer you are to your core values (your ideal self), the happier you will be when you're driving home from work every day.

Active-duty Support

If you are still on active duty, you may want to seek out your resiliency expert to leverage their expertise and resources. Their experience might help you finish the next exercise. If you've recently left active duty, you likely had other service members in your units who were there to help you with your work–life balance. They are called by different titles in each branch of service, but you may have heard them referred to as "resilience experts" or "Military and Family Life Counselors."

The Air Force's "Personnel Work-life Program" focuses on helping service members by "increasing the effectiveness of everyday living skills, learning to cope with life events and realizing one's personal potential from an increased quality of life and resilience for military members and their families." The Air Force's program helps service members to make sound decisions that will enable them to bounce back quickly from adversity and continue to be active members of their unit, family, and society. Regardless of which branch of service you served, take some time to see if you have a resiliency expert available to you.

If you've transitioned from active duty already, you can contact the National Guard Family Programs Office nearest you. Those offices are fully staffed and are there to provide transition assistance services to all branches of service. You can find the closest office by doing a simple internet search.

Real Work–Life Balance Exercise

Regardless of your current duty status, take the time to identify the key factors that impacted your work-life balance while you were on active duty and recognize how you felt about those factors. The list below identifies some factors that may have been a part of your active duty work–life balance.

Family time	Personal education	Military education
Church	Coaching kids' sports	Running
Attending kids' sports	Deployments	TDY
Family travel	Vacations	Shopping
Commuting	Fitness	Playing hockey
Skiing	Attending sporting events	Boating
Field exercises	Training	Writing
Planning	Watching TV or movies	Gaming
Fixing cars	Learning new skills	Personal health
Personal finances	Income growth	Debt reduction
Home	Office work	Maintenance work
Retirement security	Financial security	Family health

1. Think about all the factors that influenced your life when you were on active duty. Pull those factors from the list or use some ideas that you've identified on your own.

2. Write down the top three or five things that you wanted to do more.

3. Write down the top three or five things that you wished you could have done less while on active duty.

FACTORS THAT INFLUENCED MY LIFE WHILE ON ACTIVE DUTY
THINGS I WANTED TO DO MORE OF...
1.
2.
3.
4.
5.
I WISH I HAD DONE LESS OF....
1.
2.
3.
4.
5.

You've just created a picture of what your "Real Work–Life Balance" could look like. When you listed those things you wanted to do less, you likely had negative feelings about those things. And contrastingly, as you wrote about the things you wanted to do more, you likely had positive feelings about those things. This is normal and it explains how the competing interests in your life can cause joy or stress depending on what you're doing. It is surprising to see how veterans complete this exercise and discover that what they were doing on active duty didn't closely mirror their personal values.

Ideal Work–Life Balance Exercise

The factors comprising your ideal work–life balance will undoubtedly change as you shift focus from your active-duty life to your new surroundings in the civilian world. Exactly how those factors will change is completely up to you. Although you may be confronted with new pressures or obligations like securing health care coverage and learning new skills for your civilian job, you will be leaving behind old obligations and requirements as you transition out of military service. Gone will be the requirements to participate in organized physical training in the mornings. You will no longer have to fret about unscheduled deployments overseas or attend a myriad of military schools for advancement or promotion. In your new world, it will be your choice to devote your time to maintain your physical fitness or to take classes to learn a new job skill or maybe enjoy a new hobby.

Now that you have your active-duty work–life balance concepts put together, it's time to build your work–life balance sheet for what you think will be your ideal work–life balance. For this next section, you will be listing a new set of factors to help define what your work–life balance might look like in an ideal world. You can use some of the factors from your active-duty work–life balance or come up with new factors—these are the things that will be important to you in your new life.

1. Think about what you want your new life to look like and what is truly important to you in that new life.

    a. Does spending more time with family mean something to you?

    b. Do you want to be able to travel for work?

    c. Do you want to work a 9–5 job with no weekend work?

2. Write down between five and ten factors that you want to have in your new civilian life. The table below shows one example of what a list could look like. You will write these factors down on the left side of your paper or spreadsheet.

LEFT SIDE	RIGHT SIDE
Living close to family	
Spending time at home	
Traveling for work	
Taking vacations	
Saving money/investing	
Reducing debt	
Working "regular hours"	
Attending family activities (sports/plays)	
Autonomy	

Now, you need to rank the level of importance to see which ones on the list mean the most. This ranked list will help you evaluate different jobs and define the questions you might consider asking in the interview process.

3. Rank the importance of those factors on a scale of 1–10 with 1 being the least important, and the highest number (which will be somewhere between 5 and 10 on your list) as the most important. Put those rankings in the right side of your chart like this:

LEFT SIDE	RIGHT SIDE
Living close to family	6
Spending time at home	8
Traveling for work	1
Taking vacations	3
Saving money/investing	5
Reducing debt	2
Working "regular hours"	9
Attending family activities (sports/plays)	7
Autonomy	4

In the sample chart, working regular work hours is a "9" (the highest available from the list), which means the veteran doesn't want to work past five. Traveling for work is rated as a "1," which means the service member would be willing to do occasional work travel, but it's not very important if that does or doesn't happen.

Civilian Jobs and Work–Life Balance Exercise

Next, it's time to start comparing your different job prospects. Take your ranked work–life balance sheet and make copies of it. (Make as many copies as civilian positions you are considering. For example, if you have four job fields in mind, you'll make four copies of the page.)

1. On each copy, write the job title or career field at the top of the page.

2. Next to the original priority ranking, you are going to write a 1, 3, or 9. The 1 is a low value and the 9 is a high value, so if you rank the new job as a 9 for Autonomy, it means you think you will have lots of autonomy in the new career or job.

3. Once you've done that, you will multiply the two numbers together to get a final number for each category. As an example, look at the sample exercise for the category "Living close to family." You would multiply six (your level of importance for living close to family) by three (the "rating" of the family time you would have if you did financial sales for a living) and those numbers combined give you a score of eighteen.

4. Total them all up to see how your proposed job looks to you. This is your comparison of the work–life balance factors that are important to you.

By using only 1, 3, or 9, you will force a spread. This exaggeration will make important things "pop out" for you. It also will make it easier to identify negative job factors such as if a particular job might not allow you to spend time on one of your top factors.

Sample Completed Exercise: Financial Sales Rep

FINANCIAL SALES REP	
LEFT SIDE	**RIGHT SIDE**
Living close to family	6 × 3 = 18
Spending time at home	8 × 3 = 24
Traveling for work	1 × 9 = 9
Taking vacations	3 × 1 = 3
Saving money/investing	5 × 9 = 45
Reducing debt	2 × 9 = 18
Working "regular hours"	9 × 1 = 9
Attending family activities (sports/plays)	7 × 1 = 7
Autonomy	4 × 1 = 4
	Total: 137

Sample Completed Exercise: Shop Foreman

A different position for shop foreman might look something like this:

SHOP FOREMAN	
LEFT SIDE	**RIGHT SIDE**
Living close to family	6 × 9 = 54
Spending time at home	8 × 3 = 24
Traveling for work	1 × 9 = 9
Taking vacations	3 × 1 = 3
Saving money/investing	5 × 3 = 15
Reducing debt	2 × 3 = 6
Working "regular hours"	9 × 9 = 81
Attending family activities (sports/plays)	7 × 3 = 21
Autonomy	4 × 1 = 4
	Total: 217

Interpreting the Results

The samples shown in this chapter suggest that shop foreman is more compatible with your vision for work–life balance. (Look at the total scores for each position.) The samples also reveal the significant role that "spending time at home" and "working regular hours" play in the scores. If investing and reducing debt were increased in level of importance, you would expect the numbers for the financial sales representative position to score higher.

The key to this exercise is to really know the person you want to be in your next career. Be honest with yourself. The goal is to reduce the likelihood that you take a job you might be really, really good at—but absolutely hate. It turns out that former service members are comfortable in falling into a civilian job that they know how to do because they're "hitting the easy button." You're faced with the remarkable opportunity to have a fresh start, so take time and look things over to make sure you're making the right call.

To put it another way, if family time and regular work hours are incredibly important to you and you push those desires aside to take a higher paying job with lots of travel and long work hours, you run the risk of burning out and leaving in a short period of time. If you struggle here and find yourself placing a lot of emphasis on family but have an intense need or desire for higher pay (which may accompany longer hours and weekend work), there might be another option. You could put that GI Bill to work and finish your degree or learn a new skill. If you already have a degree, you could pursue a master's degree, which will put you in contention for higher salaried positions that might not have the same demands of what you would be looking at without the additional degree(s).

You can use this method to compare different types of jobs and different types of places you might want to live—the sky is the limit. The important thing is that you will be comparing your future life prospects against those things that are important to you and then make decisions that will increase the likelihood of you being a good fit in your new profession. If you pick a job or a new location that is close to your core values, it will be easier for you to balance those things in your life that are important to you. If you stray from those core values, you may find yourself having to spend more time away from those things that you value.

Feel free to go back and do this comparison as many times as you like with as many different jobs or factors as you like. You may even find it helpful to have your spouse or significant other rank each job separately just to see if you are both seeing eye-to-eye. Try it a couple different times and see if you can find what type of job might be a good fit for you.

7

ANSWERING YOUR
RESUME QUESTIONS

Joining the military was pretty easy. All you had to do was pick up the phone and call a recruiter and they took care of all the rest. Maybe the recruiter found you on social media or sent you an e-mail or even drove to your house. That's not going to be the case when you start looking for a civilian position.

To apply for almost any civilian job, you will need a resume. It's an incredibly important piece in the process of transitioning to the civilian workforce. Certainly, your actual qualifications and experience matter, but if your resume is poorly presented or badly written, you're going to have trouble getting an interview for the job you want.

Business 2 Community, an online platform for business professionals, shared some facts that might shape the way you think about preparing your resume:

- The average time a recruiter spends looking at a resume is five to seven seconds.
- 76% of resumes are discarded for an unprofessional e-mail address.
- There's an 88% rejection rate when you include a photo on your resume.

- Only 35% of applicants are actually qualified for the jobs they apply to.

- The robots that read your resume eliminate 75% of the applicants.

- Companies are increasingly using artificial intelligence to scan resumes for keywords and will discard your resume if it doesn't measure up to the job requirements. Keywords matter.

- 68% of employers will find you on Facebook.

- 89% of recruiters have hired someone through LinkedIn.

- 93% of recruiters are likely to look at a candidate's social media profile.

Steps to making your resume

1. Pick the right format and layout

2. Put your contact information at the top of the page

3. Draft your resume objective

4. List your work experience and accomplishments

5. Include your skills, training, and certifications

6. Consider additional sections like volunteering or hobbies

7. Adjust your resume for each position

8. Create a strong cover letter

9. Proofread your resume and cover letter

Why Do I Need a Resume?

A resume is a document that is commonly used in the civilian hiring process. When you're applying for a job, you can't immediately introduce yourself in person or make a personal impression, so your resume has to do the talking for you. Your resume includes information about your education, experience, and qualifications. The goal is to communicate why your skills make you right for the position in a concise, easy-to-read way. Your focus should always be on your unique qualifications that will make you a strong fit for the role.

What Format Should I Use for My Resume?

Most people use one of these three different formats for resumes:

- **Reverse chronological.** This is where you start the experience portion of your resume with your most recent position and work backwards from there. Most resumes you see are written in this format. It works really well if you have lots of work experience to list.

- **Functional.** This resume style focuses on specific skills that are most transferable to the job you're seeking. You will still include a listing of the places you've worked, but you'll list it at the end of the resume. By putting your position and title information at the end, you reduce the focus on those things, which might be beneficial when your resume is filled with military titles. Highlighting your skills first is particularly valuable when you're trying to change industries—which you are when you leave the military—and your past work job titles don't relate.

- **Combination.** If you've worked in three or four diverse areas, you will want to show that in your resume. For example, if you want to apply for a senior management role and you need skills in management, safety protocol, and logistics, you can lead with your skills and then discuss how your military experiences supported those skills.

What Needs to Be Included in My Resume?

Your resume must have the same base information as everyone else, which includes the following:

- **Contact information.** This includes your name, phone number, and e-mail address. Most people include their addresses as well, but it's certainly not required anymore. Remember, non-professional e-mail addresses get rejected.

- **Resume objective.** Write a couple of sentences about what makes you a match for the job. Some will tell you that a resume objective isn't necessary, but it's a good place to use "keywords". (See the question on "What can I do to help my resume make it past AI?" in this section.)

- **Experience.** This section shows the positions you've had in your career along with key accomplishments for each role. As a veteran, make sure you spend some time translating the military lingo into civilian phrases.

- **Education.** Here, you list any degrees or certificates you have, along with any military training. Again, when you describe your military training, focus your words on terminology that would resonate with civilian organizations (for example, leadership, teams, logistics, etc.)

- **Skills.** Create bullet points that list hard skills, such as specific software expertise, and soft skills, like communication or organization. Look for clues in the job description to match the skills listed on your resume to the needs of the organization to which you are applying.

There are optional elements, which are nice to include if you have them and have enough room, but aren't necessary to complete the resume:

- Relevant hobbies

- Languages you speak

- Volunteer work

- Special projects (especially if you had a leadership role)

- Speaking engagements or presentations

- Publications

Is There Anything that I Should Not Put on My Resume?

For the most part, you should stick to the items that are listed in the last question, but there are a few things that you'll want to avoid placing on your resume:

- **Gender, age, or marital status.** It's illegal for potential employers to ask for any of this information, so be sure to keep it off your resume. Note: That also means avoiding your high school year of graduation if you include your high school education as part of your resume.

- **Your photo.** Pictures give employers a way to make judgments based on age, gender, or race. You want your accomplishments and skills to speak for themselves. Remember, in the intro to this chapter, one study showed an 88% rejection rate when you include a photo on your resume.

- **Lies or exaggerations.** It may be tempting to include skills that match the job description, but you don't really have. If you are asked to prove any of those skills—and you can't—you will immediately lose not only that job opportunity, but also every other one at that organization.

Do I Need to Include a Resume Objective?

You don't need to include a resume objective on your resume, but it is a good place to include keywords that could help your resume get approved by the AI that will be initially reviewing your experience.

To recap, a resume objective (sometimes called a career objective) is one to three sentences that capture your short-term professional goals. They are usually placed at the top of your resume to capture the hiring manager's attention and should make your career goals clear.

What's the Best Resume Layout?

Your resume layout will be the first thing a hiring manager notices. Is it organized? Is it too short or too long? Is there too much text? Is it noticeable in the stack? Here's a checklist that you can use when you are working on your resume layout:

- **Limit the number of pages.** (See the question, "How long should my resume be?" for more information.)

- **Create clear section headings.** Use styles in Word to help keep things consistent.

- **Make sure there's lots of white space.** White space is the area on the page without print or graphics. Make sure you keep nice wide margins too.

- **Pick a font that's easy-to-read.** The font can stand out a little, but don't pick anything too strange, and avoid any fonts that look childish.

- **Use the right font size.** Most commonly, resumes use an 11 or 12-point font for normal text and a 14–16 point font for section titles.

Most people use Word to develop their resumes, but when you are done, consider saving your resume as a PDF. The PDF will make sure that your formatting does not get messed up when a hiring manager or headhunter opens it on their computer. Plus, if you used any special fonts, a PDF document will hold those too.

How Long Should My Resume Be?

There is no set length for a resume. Everyone's resume will be different depending on your experience and education. You'll hear advice that your resume should only be one page, but that is extremely difficult if you've been working for a while and if you want to leave the right amount of white space on the paper. If you are early in your career, expect to have one or two pages of content, but three pages is okay if you've got a lot of experience, accomplishments, and activities to share.

How Do I Make My Resume Stand Out?

You know your resume will be compared to many other similar applicants, so here are a few simple tips to make yours stand out:

- **Make sure there are no spelling or grammar errors.** Proofread your resume—not just once, but a bunch of times. Have a friend or coworker proof it as well. Any mistakes in your cover letter or resume label you as sloppy, and interviews are unlikely.

- **Use strong action verbs.** Your main focus will be translating your military experience into words civilians can understand. However, while you are working on that, be aware of the verbs you write down. Words like "created," "invented," or "solved" will catch the attention of your reader.

- **Keep it simple.** You've probably heard that resumes should only be one page, but that is extremely difficult if you've had a long career and/or a great deal of education. If you need more space, just add pages. What you want to avoid is making the font small or the margins narrow so it looks like you're just trying to cram everything in.

Should I Make My Resume Fancy?

Probably not. You can never go wrong with a classic, clean text document. New techniques like infographic resumes might look cooler, but unless you're applying for a graphic design, video production, or other creative role, they aren't necessary.

Additionally, think about the following when deciding what format to use:

- **Artificial Intelligence (AI) will likely be the first stop for your resume.** Online applications usually use Applicant Tracking Systems (ATS) to go over your resume before any real person will see your resume. The ATS gives employers a "match rate" that tells them if you might be a good fit. The systems look at things like "hard skills," which are skills that are developed by experience and training.

  If the technology can't read your resume, it'll just reject it. Standard text-based resumes have the best chance of making it through step one. See the question about "What can I do to help my resume make it past AI?" for more information on this topic. This is good to know for federal civilian job positions because AI will tell HR leaders not to "qualify" you for a position if you don't meet the minimum experience qualifications.

- **Most hiring managers don't have time to read resumes.** The best way to get an employer to pay attention to the content in your resume is to use a familiar format. They could get frustrated and give up if they have to spend time figuring out where to get the information they need.

How Do I Make Sure My Resume Will "Pass" the AI Review?

The filters used by an ATS to review your resume will differ depending on which system the employers are using. Fortunately, there are ways you can use AI to your advantage before you submit your resume. Use your word processor's cut-and-paste feature and move the entire job posting to a word processing document or .pdf. Do an online search for "resume match" or "resume review" to find a service that suits your needs, and then upload your resume and the job posting to see how you stack up against the competition.

You may want to try Jobscan, Resymatch, ResumeWorded, or Skillsyncher to see how your resume stands up. These services compare your resume against the job posting and provide you a report that lets you know what is missing in your resume and what you may want to add to make you more competitive. They will give you a "match rate" and tell you if your resume has the hard skills and other experience that you'll need to get your resume in front of a real person.

How Do I Translate My Military Experience into Words Civilians Would Understand?

You have spent the last several years learning to speak military. You taught your family and your friends how to speak it. Your kids know that when it's 2130, it's time to start getting ready for bed and your parents know when you're going TDY somewhere you're going to be on a work trip. The civilians who are on the other end of your e-mail will not likely understand most of this jargon. It's going to be up to you to take your military experience and break it down into plain English so that people with no military experience will want to hire you. You'll want to do this in two separate steps.

Step 1. List out all the training and schools you've attended. Start by downloading an unofficial copy of your military transcripts. The Department of Defense has a service called the Joint Services Transcript that has compiled a listing of the military courses you've taken and has identified how many semester hours of training or credit you should be able to receive if you are applying to college. Just provide a user name, your social security number, and some other information to get an instant copy of your transcripts online. Enter "Joint Services Transcript" into any search engine to get started.

Your transcripts will help you remember some of the schools you've done. This will include your basic training course, advanced training courses, and any other schools. Not all of your training may be on your transcript, but it will help you get started. For some courses, the DoD will give you a brief description of what you did in the course. Here's what the transcript explanation looks like for an Indirect Fire Infantryman for the U.S. Army:

MOSC-11C-003 Indirect Fire Infantryman	Leads or serves as a member of a mortar squad, section, or platoon...assists in construction of minor fortifications...collects and verbally reports tactical information using basic communications equipment

Once you have the list on paper or a spreadsheet, use non-military words to describe what you were doing in that school or training. You might be surprised to see that you've been taking leadership classes that started as far back as your basic training or advanced individual training. For the Indirect Fire Infantryman example, the DoD transcript shows that the mortarman had to lead at different parts of the training course. Leadership skills are highly valued at civilian organizations. As you list your military training and schools, use action words like "led" or "taught" to describe what you did in the course.

Step 2. Write down the different positions you've held in your military career. If you were enlisted, maybe you started off as a squad member and worked your way up through the ranks to be a company First Sergeant. What did you do in each of those positions? When you led a platoon of Indirect Fire Mortarmen, as the First Sergeant, what things were you responsible for doing? Again, use action words to describe what you did at each level of your career.

A First Sergeant who was responsible for her unit to deploy overseas had to rely upon not only her leadership skills to get her soldiers to do what she needed them to do, but she also had to navigate the complicated logistics system in her branch to get all the unit's equipment from her home base to her deployed location. Take some time and break down the different elements of what all goes into getting a platoon ready for such an endeavor. You will want to translate those skills, attributes, tasks, and leadership into civilian words that anyone can understand. The DoD's Joint Transcript shows that a mortarman "measures horizontal and vertical angles" and "computes firing data." Isn't that the same thing as telling someone you "used mathematical equations to solve complicated problems?"

What Can I Do to Help My Resume Make it Past AI?

As mentioned, many recruiters or potential employers use Artificial Intelligence programs to scan resumes for keywords and phrases. If your resume does not include these keywords, it will likely be rejected by the software. Applications that don't use the right keywords tend to be automatically rejected.

To make sure your resume has the right keywords and phrases, closely examine the job advertisement or job description and make a list of the words and phrases that stand out. Look for skills, activities, technology, or experiences that the description directly requests. (If there isn't a written job description, use a search engine to find ads for similar jobs and copy those keywords.) Once you've made your list, start adding those words and phrases to your resume in sections such as your resume objective, your educational history or your job experiences.

If a job posting requires "10+ years of experience in information systems management," your resume should read "14 years of experience in information systems management." If you write "10+ years of experience," the AI may not be "smart enough" to know that means you have over 10 years of experience. Also, HR leaders are on the lookout for applicants who regurgitate the job posting requirements in their resumes and are likely to discard them entirely.

Do I Need More than One Resume?

It's likely you will have more than one version of your resume so you can tailor your materials for each position you want. You might not need to change much, but you do need to make sure the items on your resume respond to the needs of the role. You should also tailor your resume to show how your work experience specifically meets the needs of each job. Here are some things to consider changing with each resume you send out:

- Edit your resume objective to focus on linking your experience and education to the organization and the specific job requirements.

- Reorder your skills to make sure the ones that are most relevant to the job are at the beginning of your resume.

- Include examples of achievements that this particular hiring manager would find impressive.

- Ensure the keywords from the job description are duplicated in your resume.

Do I Need References for My Resume?

There are mixed opinions on whether you should include references with the first copy of your resume that you submit. It's probably not a bad idea. However, if you are uncomfortable with this, then simply put "References

Available upon Request" at the bottom of your resume. The key is that you'll need to be able to produce that list immediately if a potential employer asks for your reference list.

Your reference list should list three to five people who can positively recommend you as either a person of good character or a diligent employee. Ideally, your references will be people you have worked with before. Other options include coworkers, instructors, or people you've volunteered with. It's best not to use friends or family members as a reference. Your reference list should include the name of your reference, their position title, and how they can be contacted.

Should I Put My Resume on LinkedIn?

Yes, you need to create a LinkedIn profile. If you're not familiar with the social media site, LinkedIn is the largest professional network on the planet. While looking for your new place in the civilian world, you need a LinkedIn profile that's accurate and interesting. Your LinkedIn profile is your chance to get your credentials in front of hundreds—or even thousands—of people in whichever field you choose.

LinkedIn has a number of video tutorials with instructions on how to use the site and tips on maximizing interest in your profile.

How Do I Create a Great LinkedIn Profile?

It's not enough to just have a LinkedIn page. You need a profile that draws attention, says the right things, and helps you really connect with the people you need during your transition. Here are some simple tips to improve your LinkedIn profile:

- **Add a professional picture**. This is the first impression that people will get when they look at your profile. Profiles without headshots are simply ignored.

- **Write a strong headline**. Your headline shows right below your name. Edit the default setting to make sure it really gets across what you can offer to your next employer.

- **Highlight relevant experience**. You don't need to copy your entire resume onto your profile. Online readers have short attention spans. Write a few bullets for each role that you've had with impressive and relevant accomplishments.

- **Make connections**. You need to keep growing your list of connections, including accepting the suggestions that LinkedIn makes. At this point, you never know who could end up helping you.

- **Ask for recommendations**. LinkedIn has a feature that allows people to post online comments about your work or your character. Ask a few people, like former colleagues, to write recommendations for you.

- **Stay active**. LinkedIn is a true social media site. It's just focused on professionals trying to connect. Comment on things that your network posts. Join groups where you will have automatic things in common. For example, there are a few groups focused on veterans, such as the Former U.S. Military Network which has over 12,000 members on LinkedIn.

Are There Other Social Media Platforms Where I Should Post My Resume?

While LinkedIn is the largest platform for professional networking, you should consider using as many social media sites as you can comfortably manage to support your job search. Many employers advertise jobs on Facebook. Instagram is a good way to enhance your digital presence, and you can gain insights about the places you might want to work. Twitter will allow you to talk directly to recruiters or hiring managers but because of its limited profile features, you don't want it to be the only place people can find you online. Other less common or specialized sites include Pinterest, TikTok, and YouTube. Consider these if you're looking to get into a creative field or you have multi-media content you want to share.

8

SEARCHING FOR A NEW JOB

When you are ready to search for a civilian job, you'll be experiencing a wide range of emotions. Looking for a new job can be both exciting and overwhelming. You've completed your Personal Vision statement so you know what your ideal role would look like. However, you may be anxious with all of the job hunting-related tasks, and worried when you'll actually land your next job.

Research shows that breaking down big goals into smaller, clear tasks can help make things easier. Start thinking about what your tasks might be. For example, you might send your resume out to two headhunters one week, and then have networking coffee meetings with two people during the next week. You can use the task list sample at the end of this chapter if you need a place to start.

Networking

Networking involves using personal, professional, or even family contacts to assist with learning more about an industry, or searching for a job. According to a LinkedIn survey, almost 80% of professionals consider professional networking to be important to career success. Networking can be a good way to hear about job opportunities or get connected with a specific company that interests you. If you're not sure where to begin your networking, consider contacts such as these:

- Your current colleagues and leaders
- Any members of the military you've worked with over the years
- Your classmates from any military or outside educational programs
- Friends from your personal life
- Acquaintances you know through your spouse or your family
- People from your church, gym, or community organizations
- Anyone in your world who might have information about working in the civilian world

Tips for Networking

- **Be deliberate in selecting people.** Think carefully about who can assist you in finding a civilian job. If you are moving to a new area, join some groups to meet as many people as possible. Even if you haven't been in touch with someone for a while, you can use the opportunity to catch up and tell them about your career plans. Don't be shy about reaching out to family and friends. You never know who might have a connection that will help.

- **Network online.** Sites like LinkedIn, Facebook, and other social media can help you get in touch with people at specific companies, or who live in a certain part of the country. Look for groups that you can join, which would connect you to people that have common interests or some other connection (like education). Keep in mind that when you are reaching out to people you don't know, be sure you know exactly what you want and be detailed in asking for it.

- **Be prepared to give something back.** Networking isn't a one-way street. Once you meet or chat with someone, plan on sharing an interesting article based on what you discussed. Or maybe they are looking for a new job opportunity too, so you can share what you find during your job search. The point of having a network is to connect with people who can help you, but you should reciprocate whenever you can.

- **Keep track of your network.** Whether you use a spreadsheet, an app, or simply write it down in a notebook, make sure you know who you reached out to, how you connected with them, and how to get in touch in the future. You might even want to make a couple notes about personal information, such as a spouse's name or pets, so you can easily remember those details when you reach out again.

- **Attend networking events.** It can be uncomfortable at first, but networking in person does work. Community groups or professional associations often hold meetings or mixers, or you could consider a social group like a car club or sports enthusiasts. Many attendees at these in-person events are also looking for career opportunities and will be glad to exchange contact information. Consider having some business cards created with your personal phone number and e-mail address to make it easy for people to contact you. And be sure to do some follow up with the people you met after the event is over.

Headhunters

A headhunter is a company (or sometimes an individual) that provides recruiting services on behalf of the employer. Generally, headhunters are hired by organizations to locate and contact people who meet specific job requirements. While this book should not be considered an endorsement of any particular headhunting firm, the dissertation research showed that headhunting firms increase chances for veteran placement and improve retention rates of veterans.

Half of the former military members who were interviewed for the dissertation used a headhunter to find their first job after leaving the military. In all of these cases, the veterans said they "fit in" with their new position and planned on staying several years. In each case, the veterans were placed in leadership roles with organizations in the defense industry. These employers recognized the skills and experience of those veterans based on their military service. In other words, these employers "got it."

By working with a headhunter, the veterans got jobs in a field that was similar to what they experienced while on active duty. Their new jobs had a defined hierarchy, a clear path for career progression, and an integrated mission and purpose. One military intelligence officer who now runs a civilian robotics team said, "You're at least getting back into the same culture...the same worlds."

Headhunters have a real and true interest in ensuring the veteran is a good fit for a civilian position. Remember, headhunters don't get paid unless they are able to place a person in a job in which they end up staying for a certain period (normally a year). The dissertation research showed that headhunters made the transition easier for veterans by matching veterans with jobs that have similar work cultures to what the veteran left behind. Plus, the headhunters aimed to put veterans into organizations that valued their skills. One veteran who was part of the study commented, "I definitely think they value [my military experience]. There's the experience of leading teams and finding solutions that they respect."

The headhunters also made the interviewing process easier for the veterans by putting the person looking for a job in direct touch with hiring decision makers. One interviewed soldier remarked, "I was interviewing directly with the people who would be hiring me instead of being guided to a lot of steps for the HR process." All of these extra support services can really help the transition to civilian life.

Tips for Choosing a Headhunter

- **Consider using a headhunter who works with former members of the military.** There are a number of headhunting firms that specialize in placing veterans. A quick Google search will bring up some of the most popular ones. The other way to approach the decision is to choose a headhunter that specializes in the industry you want to work in. For example, if you know (based on your values exercise and personal vision statement) that you want to teach as a civilian, there are headhunters who specialize in educational jobs.

- **Ask what other services they provide.** In addition to bringing you information about job openings, many headhunters offer services to get you ready for the process. For example, some will review your resume and cover letter to offer suggestions and changes. Some will conduct mock interviews so you are prepared for this step. And some will have tools to help you negotiate a top-notch total compensation package. Understand what the headhunter offers so you can compare firms and make a choice that matches what help you need.

- **Interview the recruiter.** First, you will select the headhunting firm, and then they will assign you at least one recruiter to work with. This recruiter is going to be an important relationship for your transition and you should be sure it's going to work. Ask about the recruiter's background, including how long he or she has been with this headhunter. Be sure you understand how the process will work and the timing you can expect for results. In the end, there certainly needs to be a personality fit or you won't see many of the benefits of working with this recruiter.

- **Check the recruiter's references.** Don't be embarrassed to ask the recruiter for references. Talk to current and former clients about the services and what they thought of working with this recruiter. Be sure to ask if the reference would use this recruiter again. You will learn a lot from those answers.

Remember that using a headhunter should only be one step in your search for a civilian job. That means you should not stop your own job search efforts, and let your recruiter know that you are continuing to seek your own opportunities. See the other sections in this chapter for more information about networking and online job hunting.

Online Job Hunting

Long gone are the days where a jobseeker had to wait for the Sunday newspaper to look for help-wanted ads. You no longer have to buy postage stamps to mail your cover letter and resume to potential employers. Rather, online job searches are common practices. Your best option will always be combining an online job search with networking and direct contact with potential employers. This section covers the pros and cons of using the Internet to find employment.

Advantages

- Most online applications are simple and some even allow you to just upload your resume and cover letter with no additional forms to complete

- Appeals to job seekers who want to apply for as many jobs as possible

- Convenience of searching for jobs at any time of the day or night

- Delivers cost savings because the only expense you might have is transportation to an in-person interview (though sometimes, employers pay for candidate travel expenses as well)

- Access to information about jobs you never knew existed, especially if you are interested in moving to a new part of the country

Disadvantages

- Impersonal application process that often uses Artificial Intelligence to screen out candidates

- Provides too many options that may cause you to be overwhelmed at the number of possible job opportunities

- Challenge to keep track and follow up on the high volume of applications you may submit

- High-level organizational positions are not often posted online. Networking is your best option to find these types of roles.

- Scams can be disguised as job openings to gain access to your personal information so be sure to use reliable websites and sources

Popular Online Job Search Resources for Veterans

WEBSITE	OWNERSHIP	DESCRIPTION (*SUPPLIED BY THE WEBSITES*)
Indeed.com	Independent operating unit of Japan-based Recruit Co. Ltd.	Job search site that provides special resources for transitioning service members, such as job search boot camp, resume review, and career advice from a large library of articles.
LinkedIn for veterans	Microsoft Corporation, publicly traded multinational technology company	Connects military members to opportunities by giving you the tools to build your professional brand, manage your network, and gain new skills. Eligible members of the U.S. military community receive one year of LinkedIn Premium where you can get unlimited access to more than 10,000 courses on the LinkedIn Learning platform.

Military.com	Monster Worldwide, publicly traded provider of employment services such as Monster.com	Provides news and information about benefits to military members, veterans, and their families. Search free veteran jobs board, find jobs with military-friendly companies, build and post your civilian resume and network with veterans to make the most out of your military skills and experience in the civilian world.
RecruitMilitary.com	Bradley Morris, privately held military and staffing agency	RecruitMilitary connects employers to military job seekers through services that include career fairs, a job board, and a military-centric magazine. Services are free of charge to the military community.
USAJOBS.com	U.S. federal government, US Office of Personnel Management (OPM)	Federal agencies use USAJOBS to host job openings and match qualified applicants to those jobs. USAJOBS serves as the central place to find opportunities in hundreds of federal agencies and organizations.

This information on online recruiting is supplied by the websites them-selves and is up-to-date, as of the publishing date of this book. However, please note that, as has been mentioned, being listed as a resource in this chapter does not constitute or imply its endorsement, recommendation, or favoring by the authors or publishers of this book.

Interviewing

One of the most nerve-wracking parts of the job search for some people is the inevitable interview. The answer for this anxiety comes down to preparation. Everyone knows this, but few people do enough homework to prepare for each interview. Find out as much as possible about the organization—how and why it was formed, what are its financial results, what do people say about its culture. Research the industry looking for trends and challenges.

Don't forget to get to know as much as possible about each of the people you will meet during the interview. Finally, read the job description over and over, so that you can show that you have what it takes to fill the role. Focus particularly on how your experiences in the military have prepared you for the most important requirements listed for the job. Most interviewers won't have a natural understanding of your military responsibilities, so you need to translate what you did into how it fits in the civilian workplace. This might take some practice so be open to doing mock interviews with friends or family members so you can get this part right.

Plan for Remote Interviews

Since online meeting platforms have really taken off, it's possible that the first few rounds of interviews with your prospective boss and colleagues will not happen in person. If you're doing a video interview, you'll want to take extra steps to get familiar with the technology and set up a professional-looking background. Because you won't get as much non-verbal feedback during the conversation, focus on conveying warmth and establishing an emotional connection. Keep in mind: Your voice matters more in video than it does in-person.

Pick Your Top Three Messages

Before you interview for any job, decide what messages you want to get across to the interviewer. Focus on making the connection between what you've accomplished in your military career and training and what's needed in the role. As you work on these messages, start with the idea that the interviewer has needs that he or she wants met. To put it simply, they want their lives to be easier by hiring someone. They would also like the person to be up-and-running at the job tasks as quickly as possible and be relatively pleasant to work with. Consider these questions and statements to help you prepare your top three messages.

STATEMENT	PURPOSE
I am highly interested in this role.	It makes the process much easier when you come right out and say that you are interested in the job. The interviewer knows that they don't have to spend a lot of time selling you on the organization or the job, and can spend more time getting to know you and your qualifications. Everyone wants to be liked, and you just told that interviewer that you like his or her organization and job. It's a good place to start.
I did my home-work and I know this organization pretty well.	Share some insights and knowledge that you gathered about the organization. You can also ask questions about the organization's mission, operations, or results. It all shows that you are genuinely interested in the organization and aren't just picking places to interview at random.

I know the backgrounds of the people in this room with me.	You aren't stalking if you go to the LinkedIn profiles of the people who will be at your interview to see their backgrounds. Keep in mind that when you check out a LinkedIn profile, the person you are researching knows that you accessed their information. That's not bad—it could even really work in your favor. The interviewers will know that you came to the interview prepared.
How can I best help you in this job?	Which manager wouldn't want to hear that from a prospective employee? This question could also reveal so much about what the manager wants, which means you'd know what you'd be doing on most days.
Thank you for taking the time for this interview. I appreciated learning more about the organization and the role and look forward to continuing conversations with you.	Thank you is always a good way to end the discussion. Plus, you can go on to say how you believe that your experience and skills can help the organization. Make sure you offer to provide anything else that could help them with their decision.

Practice the Common Interview Questions

Many job interviewers take a fairly common approach to interview questions. Here are some of the most common interview questions, along with thoughts on how to prepare for the trickiest ones.

- **Tell me about yourself**

  Don't just repeat the information that's in your resume or cover letter. Instead, tell a couple of short stories that match the organization's values, or what the job calls for. For example, if organization values innovation, share a couple things that you've innovated in both your military role and your personal life.

- **What are your strengths?**

  Provide a clear and direct answer to this question. And it's not about just telling them your strengths, it's about proving them. Therefore, provide at least one example for each of the strengths you list. For example, if you are amazing at organizing large amounts of data, tell the interviewer how you made a difference doing just that in one of your military assignments.

- **What is your greatest weakness?**

  You're not being tricked with this question. Rather, the interviewer is really just trying to discover if you have self-awareness. They also want to know if you're able to tell the truth, even when it's uncomfortable, so just be honest. Choose something that you could genuinely improve and explain what you've done to improve in this area and how you'll continue.

- **Where do you see yourself in five years?**

  There are so many better questions that an interviewer can ask, but this one still seems to come up quite often. Some candidates will try to show incredible ambition, or they will try to be humble. A unique answer is where you try to craft something that shows your dreams, your interests, and highlights the kinds of people you want to work with. Take a little extra time to prepare for this super common (and somewhat annoying) question.

- **What do you see as your greatest accomplishment?**

  Make sure you have an answer that would obviously relate to the job you want. For example, if you say that your greatest accomplishment was recruiting more soldiers than anyone else in a year, but you are applying for a middle school teaching job, your answer may be interesting but not relevant. Look through the job description and choose some of your accomplishments that would directly apply to the role. The goal is to share achievements that help the interviewer imagine you succeeding at their organization.

- **What kind of culture do you like to work in?**

  The word culture is likely to be tossed around in an interview. But since you've already done your values exercise and your personal vision, you should have a good answer to this. In particular, because you shouldn't be interviewing for any organization or any job that isn't already aligned with what you want. When you answer this question, find ways to highlight how the organization's environment matches with your values. And if you can't—walk away—because you won't last long there anyway.

- **Tell me about a tough decision you've made in the last year.**

For a veteran, this question can be tricky. The decisions you may have had to make lately are not the kind of decisions most civilians have faced. So you might want to consider toning it down although you definitely need to have at least one good answer. Having no answer is a red flag. A good answer will show how you can make a decision using data and facts. A great answer will demonstrate how you dealt with the people and any conflict that may have developed from your decision.

- **What is your leadership style?**

This question can catch people off-guard because the first thought you have is trying to come up with a label for your style. Instead, try sharing stories about how you handled leadership situations. Simply say, "I'd like to explain my style by giving you a few examples of leadership challenges I've faced." And then tell your stories. Think about situations in which you dealt with a problem, motivated a team, or worked through a crisis. Remember to pick examples that a civilian will understand. Every organization does training, has conflicts among team members, or faces dissatisfied customers. Explain exactly what you did in one of those situations and that will give the interviewer a solid understanding of how you lead.

- **Tell me about how you handled a situation where you disagreed with your leader's decision**.

For veterans, this question may be difficult. As a veteran, you've likely had your own opinion about how different tasks or orders should have been carried out, but weren't in a position to do anything about it because you were junior in rank and pretty much had to do what you were told. You'll want to think about a situation where you disagreed with how something was executed and talk about how you might have influenced things to go a little more smoothly. Be careful in the language you are using if you're talking about a combat operation. You don't want to overwhelm your interviewer by using language that reflects what you had to do in a combat situation. The most important thing is to show that you remained calm and professional while raising your concerns in a productive way. The question for you is if you are willing to be honest, to share concerns and issues, but to also get behind a decision and support it as if you agreed, even if you didn't. You should know your true answer before you are ever asked the question.

- **What do you like to do when you aren't working?**

Some organizations will use outside interests as a way to determine how you will fit into the organization or into the team. Don't try to make up things and say that you enjoy hobbies you don't. Focus on unique interests, or activities that show skills you're trying to learn. Maybe share an exciting story from your last 5K race, or describe the most recent book you've read. Plus, since you've done some personal exploration recently, you could discuss hobbies you want to start. You might tee it up with, "I've spent the last few years balancing my military service and my family, so I'm really looking forward to coaching my son's soccer team, and volunteering at the food bank once a month."

Evaluate the Organization

Remember that your interview isn't all about selling yourself. It's also an opportunity to evaluate the organization and compare the culture to your identified values. In other works, is this workplace right for you?

Pay attention to how the manager and other interviewers treat you throughout the process. Are they open and welcoming? Did you get a good feeling about him or her? Can you picture yourself working with this individual, particularly when it comes to solving problems or tackling challenging situations?

It may be tempting to simply ask, "How would you describe the culture at this organization?" However, there are more targeted questions that you can ask to help assess whether the organizational culture will be a good fit for you. Consider some of these:

- What makes you proud to work at this organization?

- When someone makes a mistake on a project, how does your team handle that?

- How are problems resolved when one department does not agree with another department's approach?

- How does the organization keep everyone on the same page when there are some people who work remotely?

- What's the one thing you would change about the organization if you could?

Finally, review Chapter 11 about Civilian Pay and Benefits for examples of questions you can ask about the organization's total compensation package. You might want to consider saving some of these questions until a second or third interview, but it's good to have a strong understanding of civilian pay and benefits terms before you meet with a prospective employer.

Sample Job Search Task List

TASKS	TIMELINE
PREPARING A PLAN	
Develop a schedule setting key tasks and deadlines	Week 1
Complete personal vision statement to refine search parameters (including type of work and location)	Weeks 1–5
Gather information on industries and search resources	Weeks 6–8
List search options, including networking and headhunters	Weeks 9–10

Gather data for resume, including military assignments, awards, education, etc.	Weeks 1–10

CREATING DOCUMENTATION

Create initial resume	Weeks 11–12
Draft a cover letter that can be edited for different positions	Weeks 11–12
Have resume reviewed and edited by multiple sources	Weeks 13–15
Have a professional picture taken for social media	Weeks 13–15
Create profiles on selected social media sites	Weeks 16–18

SEARCHING FOR A JOB

Create list of networking contacts	Weeks 20–21
Create system for tracking networking contacts	Week 22
Meet with two networking contacts each week	Ongoing
Contact headhunting firm	Weeks 22–23
Locate appropriate networking events	Weeks 22–23
Participate in networking events	Ongoing
Identify online job-hunting resources	Weeks 24–26
Upload information to selected job-hunting sites	Weeks 26–29

PREPARING FOR INTERVIEWING

Buy appropriate interview clothing	Immediately
Prepare at least three key messages	Weeks 30–31
Write down answers to common interview questions	Weeks 32–34
List questions you want to ask during interview	Weeks 35–36
Research organization	1 week prior
Research interviewers	1 week prior
Prepare thank you communications	1 day after

9

USING CULTURE TO YOUR ADVANTAGE

The research shows that culture is the primary reason veterans leave their first civilian jobs at such high rates. Veterans have been living in a strictly regimented society where rules and regulations are everywhere. The Army even has a manual that tells you how to dig a latrine in the field. Your ability to live in the military world depended on your ability to understand all the written and unwritten rules and then make decisions within that set of rules. So, how do you successfully move from that environment into the civilian workforce that has extreme cultural differences depending on what organization you join?

If you aren't sure how culture can affect your daily world, here is a story about Jay who was just trying to get a cup of coffee in a place with cultural differences. When Jay was TDY in the Virgin Islands, he was surprised that all the locals would give the greeting of the day every time they walked into a room or a restaurant. It didn't matter if they knew the people in the restaurant or not. They always said "Hello"—to everybody. One morning when Jay walked into a local restaurant, groggy from working late, he forgot to say "Good morning" when he ordered his coffee. He just walked up to the counter and asked for a coffee with cream and a little sugar. The first cup of coffee he was handed was black, so he asked them to add cream and sugar. The second cup of coffee had cream—way too much cream. By the third cup of coffee, Jay understood that his lack of a "Good morning" greeting offended the restaurant employee. The coffee order was unlikely to be correct from this point forward.

Why did this coffee mishap happen? Jay wasn't playing within the cultural rules. He needed to say "Good morning" before he ordered his coffee. Being able to operate within the cultural norms plays a key role in determining how you will fit in with the work culture and the non-work culture where you are going. In Jay's case, he didn't get the cup of coffee he wanted, but it's easy to see how a simple miscalculation in navigating work culture can make it challenging for veterans to get even the most simplistic work tasks done.

Culture refers to those tangible and intangible aspects of life that influence behavior, and consists of such elements as:

- Language
- Values
- Knowledge (individual and collective)
- Assumptions
- Expectations
- Beliefs (including religion)
- Rituals

Sometimes, it's easy to spot the elements of culture and sometimes the signs are a little more subtle. For example, if you grew up in the Midwest in the eighties and lived near a steel mill, car plant, or a coal mine, you and your neighbors probably drove a car that was made in the United States. The "Buy American" slogan was powerful and as a result, mid-Westerners developed a culture of purchasing U.S. products. Of course, if you strayed too far from "Buy American" and bought a foreign car, you may have been asked to park your car on the street instead of in your girlfriend's driveway.

Cultural Friction

Jay's inability to grab a quick cup of coffee on his TDY trip happened because he ignored the social rules in the Virgin Islands. Jay's conduct created something called "cultural friction." Cultural friction is like having a rock in your boot during a road march. At first, the rock seems like a small thing, but it can completely derail your ability to perform. When you first notice the rock in your boot, you're better off taking care of it immediately.

When the research points to culture as the reason active-duty service members leave their civilian jobs, it means "cultural friction," or the chaffing caused when the service member isn't able to operate within the social framework of their new environment.

Some people are really good at "reading the room" and are able to quickly understand what the social rules might be in any given situation. Those people typically fit in pretty quickly when they move into a new environment. They have a high degree of what's called Emotional Intelligence (EI). EI (sometimes called emotional quotient or EQ) is the ability to understand, manage, and use your emotions in positive ways. Masters of EI can communicate effectively, empathize with others, overcome challenges, and reduce conflict. Emotional intelligence can help you build stronger relationships and achieve your career and personal goals. A high degree of EI will enable you to understand your new work environment.

Types of Capital

When you were on active duty, you had several different types of status. Maybe you were an expert in running the targetry system for naval gunnery, but were lower ranking than most of the other people on your team. If you knew more about how the systems worked, your expert-level experience likely gave you a little more sway with your coworkers and supervisors. This knowledge was a commodity that you could use as leverage to project "above your pay grade." As a gunnery expert, you were able to influence up because you knew how the weapon system worked better than your superiors, and in doing so you might have gained an elevated social status because of that knowledge. Social scientists would say that you were able to influence up due to the capital you held in the area of naval gunnery.

Capital is the currency people use to interact with other people as they navigate through different fields in society. We operate in many different fields. Work is a field. Participating in a hobby such as a book club or as a goalie in the Over-30 Hockey League are all different fields. Maybe you participate actively in your church group. Your church group and all the activities that surround it are another field where you use your capital to engage in those activities.

In your active-duty military world, your fields likely interacted with one another and were integrally meshed. When you saw your commanding officer off-post at a Starbucks, you still called her Ma'am and extended her military courtesies. Maybe you lived on post/base and were surrounded with other active-duty service members and their dependents 24/7. Baby showers and birthday parties all took place inside your military bubble. And in that bubble, your rank, military education, military skills, and deployment experience all played roles in determining where you stood socially and what you were able to get done.

While a Major still will be a Major on base and on the Over-30 Hockey League and even at the Starbucks off base, it won't mean the same thing in the civilian world. In the civilian world, veterans' fields won't overlap as much. Work will be work. Hockey league will be a separate and distinct group outside of work. Church group will unlikely overlap with work or hockey. Because veterans' civilian worlds won't operate the same way they did in the military bubble, veterans often struggle in being able to transfer their capital from one field into another. Initially, post active-duty life feels more segregated and fractured. This is because veterans don't walk around with their rank in their back pocket.

It's important to understand different types of capital that people use to make their way through the world and reach their goals:

- **Symbolic Capital.** Symbolic capital refers to the honor, prestige, or recognition that someone might hold in their societal groupings or fields. When a Congressional Medal of Honor recipient walks into a room to give a speech, everybody claps. Civilians recognize this level of symbolic capital. A flag officer rank creates a high social standing both in the military realm and in the civilian world. Everybody knows that a Vice Admiral or a Major General had to do some incredibly skillful things for a long time to attain that rank. Service academy grads bring a higher standing with them when they leave active duty because as soon as they say "West Point" or the "Naval Academy" in a job interview, the interview panel will undoubtedly relax and start asking questions about their time at the academy.

- **Social capital.** Social capital refers to the different social networks that individuals will have to navigate during their day-to-day lives. Some of these networks interact with one another in a way that allows the individual's capital to transfer from one network to another. When you were on active duty, you may have joined a military friendly organization like the Military Officer's Association, or the Association of the United States Army. If you went to one of their meetings or maybe an annual convention, you would have been surrounded by a bunch of people just like you who understood what it means to be a Sergeant Major or a Navy O-6. There, your social capital converted directly and easily and it was that capital that allowed you to really enjoy the conference. On active duty, you likely had a network of family members and friends who were always asking how you and your dependents were doing. You may have been a practicing member of your church or synagogue or mosque. Any participation, membership, or inter-action you had with things outside of work (Scouting, your kids' T-ball league, or even a book club) all make up your social capital.

- **Political capital.** When Lindsey Graham, an Air National Guard Colonel, took a couple briefings in Afghanistan in 2010–2011, the Navy three-star called him "Sir" during the briefing. Why was that? Colonel Graham was also a United States Senator at the time. The Vice Admiral was calling Colonel Graham Sir because Colonel Graham had political capital as Senator Graham.

Cultural Capital in Action

Cultural capital is the ability of an individual to use their different types of capital and apply it as they shift through their different social fields. The targetry expert in the beginning of this chapter had a high degree of cultural capital because he knew all there was to know about the targeting system he was controlling. For *The Hunt for Red October* (1990) fans, when Jack Ryan went into the situation room to explain that a Russian nuclear submarine commander wanted to defect to the United States instead of starting World War III, he used his cultural capital. The Chairman of the Joint Chiefs had him surely on symbolic capital as the highest ranking person in the room, but Jack Ryan was the man of the hour because nobody knew the submarine commander better than Ryan did—cultural capital.

Cultural capital is made up of the social tools that an individual uses to get things done in their environments. You use your cultural capital toolkit every day, but it's unlikely that you ever really think about it. Your cultural capital toolkit includes how smart you are at particular things, how you talk, your military and civilian education, and how you present yourself to other people through your demeanor and even the clothes you're wearing. We use our cultural capital toolkit to help us navigate our way through a day at work or at a baseball game with the kids.

By this point, you may be asking yourself, "How can I take this capital that I may have to make it easier for me to transition?" The trick is being able to figure out how you can take your skills, training, experience, social standing, and education and use it all in the civilian world so you can increase the likelihood that you will be able to play well with others. If you can translate or transfer your capital from your military world to your civilian world, you will find it easier to maneuver through work and home. Remember, studies show that service members who have and maintain strong social networks will have much higher chances of having a smooth transition from active duty life to the civilian world.

Translating Capital

You've done a lot in your military career when you really think about it. If you're enlisted, you completed basic training, and advanced military training in your particular skill. If you're an officer, you did your basic course and graduated from your advanced course after you learned the basics of what you needed to know in your branch. If you reached the rank of E-5 or higher, you attended additional leadership training that civilian organizations would love to have their managers to have attended—they just don't know it yet. If you made it to a field grade officer, you have attended a senior leadership course that civilian organizations typically reserve for their top 10% of managers—they just don't know it yet.

The civilian world calls these employees with advanced leadership training "High Potentials" (or HIPOs) because they have high potential for future leadership. These are the employees who become managers, senior managers, vice presidents, and Chief Operating Officers—maybe people like you.

In 2022, Amazon had a special pre-executive program called the Pathways Program. As a Pathways participant, the veteran starts as an area manager and matriculates through different leadership phases in the five-year program. At the end of the fifth year, many Pathways participants make it to the general manager level. Initial Pathways employees usually start at $130,000/year while general managers are paid close to $250,000 annually. Amazon recognizes the leadership skills that military personnel bring with them and is actively seeking them out. Amazon's five-year program helps veterans learn how to adjust their leadership skills to the civilian workplace. The problem is that not every company has this kind of vision when hiring veterans.

This is where the capital conversion process comes in. In the civilian world, companies only send their top candidates to leadership courses. You might have graduated from a military program that was as good as (or better than) those civilian leadership courses. While companies like Amazon and Northrop Grumman understand what they're getting when they hire a veteran, mid-sized businesses (500–10,000 employees) and small businesses (5–500 employees) generally don't recognize the leadership skills that veterans might bring to their organization. They know they want to hire veterans, but HR leaders in civilian organizations often can't even describe the difference in skill level or leadership capabilities of an E-4 compared to an O-4—a veteran is a veteran.

Keep in mind that other candidates for the role you want may have never completed the rigorous training that you have done to develop leadership skills. The problem is your future employer may have absolutely no idea what that means to their bottom line. So it's your job to explain how your skills and training can help them. You'll need to do this in your resume, during your interview, and you'll need to continue to reinforce it all once you get hired into your dream job.

Recognizing the Differences

It's time to come to grips with some of the differences you will experience at work that will, at times, make you think back to the good-old days when military rank and military titles made everything so easy. When veterans experience some of these differences, they sometimes feel out of place in their new environment. Recognizing these differences before you apply or interview for a civilian role can help you prepare for the path forward.

Rank	Get comfortable with people calling you by your first name. You'll be calling your coworkers and bosses by their first name as well. It might feel disrespectful at first, but you'll get used to it.
Formality	Civilian organizations are usually pretty informal. Be prepared for everything to feel a little more relaxed.
Timeliness	Meetings don't always start on time and projects aren't always done on time.
Team/unit/cohesion	You may not have the same feeling of unity or cohesion in your work group. There is no military mission to intensely connect the group.
Respect	You will have to earn everyone's respect. You can't carry your rank in your back pocket and pull it out when you need it.
Speech	You will have to learn how people talk to each other in your workplace. Every work group is different, and you can't "assert your dominance" because you might be a subject matter expert.
Sense of Purpose	Many of your coworkers will be just working at a job. Some of the people may be working for a purpose, but you won't likely feel the same sense of unity or drive in your new civilian position. It's hard to go from defending your nation to defending a profit margin.

Converting Capital

It's clear that your ability to transfer your capital to your civilian world will significantly impact how you will fit in at work, and how successfully you will be able to function as a leader. Here are some factors of how your capital will enable you to influence your future environment.

- **Be prepared to feel a little lost.** One transitioning soldier in the research study commented, "You can't walk around with your rank in your back pocket." When you transition from active duty to civilian life, your rank doesn't come with you. Unless you are an academy graduate or a transitioning flag officer, it's pretty unlikely that the status you had in the military will transfer to your new role at most civilian organizations. Addressing this loss can be a big challenge. You will likely experience a feeling of loss when you move away from your life of rigid rules and procedures, a defined rank structure, and a system of social rules and values. The intensity and degree that you will experience this loss of your social capital will be individual to you.

- **Expand or create new networks.** You relied on many different social networks during your active-duty career. They helped you deal with adversity and were there with you to celebrate your many successes. Spend some time reinforcing the networks that you already have so you can rely upon them when you leave active duty. Build new networks if needed. Look for military social groups where you plan on retiring. Contact the Morale Wellness and Recreation or Family Support Groups close to where you are moving. Their job is to help service members like you fit in with your new surroundings. Joining and participating in new clubs or organizations is a fun and easy way to meet other people who have similar interests. There's an entire new world out there that is definitely worth exploring.

Join veterans' advocacy groups

Consider joining a veterans' advocacy group. Organizations like the American Legion, Veterans of Foreign Wars, Military Officers Association, and the Association of the United States Army can provide you with people and services to help your transition. The Military Officers Association has a transition assistance program tailored to help officers transition from active duty. Some veterans find that having a place they can go and just hang out to watch a football game can be incredibly grounding. If you're in Annapolis, Maryland, swing by the Fleet Reserve Club and you'll easily see the esprit de corp spilling out from its doors overlooking Ego Alley.

Boost Your Cultural Capital

While not much of your symbolic capital will make the trip with you, you can do a lot to increase your cultural capital before you leave active-duty so it's there to rely on as you reach your new destination. Build on your current cultural capital to meet the needs you will have when you've transitioned. How do you do this?

- **Start early**. Ideally, you are thinking about your exit strategy around thirty-six months before you ETS. There's a lot to do. You need to find a place where you and your family want to live, research possible industries or roles, and pick a type of job that aligns with your values. Maybe you would benefit from enrolling in some certification courses or schools so you can compete at the same level of your civilian peers. Some of those courses have enrollment requirements and can take a year or more to finish. It's never too late to get things going. The important thing is to keep reminding yourself that you're going to be competing with civilians who have probably come with considerable job or industry experience.

- **Harness your intellect.** Intellect is an individual's ability to receive different bits of information and use reason to reach "correct" decisions objectively. Throughout your military career, you've been using your critical thinking skills to look at a problem. Still, "harnessing your intellect" means thinking a little differently when you're confronted with a problem. Spend more time brainstorming solutions because you can't "pull rank" or rely on your experience as you guess your way to success. You can improve your intellectual prowess by working on Sudoku puzzles, playing chess, and practicing math problems. Reading challenging books and learning a new language can help increase your intellectual capacity as well. Focus your reading on the area of business where you want to work. Stay current with the events that are going on in that business and keep a journal. Read the news every day and see what's new. If you're looking for a job in finance, banking, or insurance, it's probably a good idea to know what the Federal Reserve has been up to the past twenty-four months.

- **Keep your network close.** Do your best to keep ties with those people who mean something to you. You can talk to your battle buddy or First Sergeant before you leave active duty and get a commitment from them to have some type of contact every two weeks or maybe once a month. We talk about the importance of engaging with or creating civilian Veterans Affinity Groups in Chapter 10. There might even be a benefit in creating a Veterans Affinity Group while you're still on active duty and getting ready to transition. You're all going through the same thing and could help each other work through transition issues.

- **Learn the language**. Chapter 5 addressed this in great detail, but it's important to see how language influences a person's ability to integrate with a new group. Imagine joining an over thirty soccer league as a goalie but that you didn't know any of the soccer rules. Your athletic ability might make you feel ready to go, but if you don't have the ability to "fit" with the team, understand the rules, and know how to interact with the referees, you will struggle. The same thing applies to your new coworkers and supervisors. Your "language" is noticed very early in the process. The e-mail address you used to send in your resume matters. Punctuation matters too. You can start learning the language in the earliest phases of your transition.

- **Promote your education.** When you were on active duty, you competed against your peers for promotions, and that was based on a variety of different factors. Education was most certainly one of them. Fortunately, education is something that you can use to your advantage to make yourself stand out from other candidates. Take some time researching appealing industries or fields to see what kind of backgrounds and education are required. Compare what you've learned in your military schools so you can highlight how competitive you are as a candidate.

1. Consider a civilian's career from the first entry-level position all the way to the level of position you're interested in seeking. What would a civilian employee have experienced and learned to get to that level in their profession?

2. Write down all the attributes that individual would have developed to get to where you want to go (skills/training/formal education).

3. Next to each one of attributes, note how long it would take to achieve those skills (six months, four years, etc.)

4. On a second sheet of paper, write down all the military schools and training you've completed to get to where you are.

5. Include the number of people you supervised over your career at each different stage and briefly describe what it is that you were doing at the time.

If you see any big gaps between you and the skills/education that are required for the position you'd like to have, decide if it makes sense to enroll in a certification course or take classes to finish an Associate's degree, Bachelor's degree or a Master's. Do you want to work in the Homeland Security field? The Federal Emergency Management Agency's Center for Domestic Preparedness has over fifty certification courses available. Maybe you could set aside five or ten hours every week and work on a course online.

10

JOINING OR FORMING
A VETERAN'S AFFINITY GROUP

The dissertation research led to the conclusion that veterans' affinity groups increase retention in a civilian organization. To understand why affinity groups can be successful, it is important to recognize that if you, as a veteran, find a civilian job that acknowledges your military leadership skills, training, and experience, you can leverage those experiences to fit in and to grow in your new civilian workplace. It will make it easier for you to leverage your military capital and use it to help you get done what you need to get done at work because your supervisors and coworkers will have a better understanding of how awesome you really are.

Veterans' affinity groups build strong bonds and connect veterans to their new community. They can give you a place to share common experiences, which builds deep connections and helps you integrate into the new culture. In one of the dissertation interviews, an HR leader explained how veterans at her organization "are lacking in their experience in transitioning from military to civilian worlds." She said that one of the things the employees who had former military experience would tell her is that they missed the "connection to community." She acknowledged that civilian organizations really needed to connect with veterans and say, "can we help make some introductions for you? What are your interests? What do you like to do outside of work?" That's exactly what a veterans' affinity group could be designed to do.

Any civilian organization—regardless of size or budget—could encourage its employees to develop a veterans' affinity group. Providing a place where veterans can share their experiences, and work together on company and community issues, could reduce turnover and create an incredible culture where veterans are set up to succeed.

What Is an Affinity Group?

An affinity group is simply a group of people who share a common interest or goal, or they want to come together for a specific purpose. Sometimes they are called an Employee Resource Group (ERG) or an Employee Network Group (ENG).

Affinity groups are voluntary and employee-driven so you can expect that any gatherings or events will be planned by someone in the group. The group usually provides support and networking opportunities, including things like networking, career development, and community outreach. Most importantly, they provide a way for employees with something in common to gather, make friends, and share ideas.

If you join a veterans' affinity group, you will benefit from having a small, tight-knit community that can focus on issues that are important to you. In many situations, your affinity group works with a wide variety of leaders at your organization to actually improve how things are done, including new programs or initiatives that could make it easier for your veteran colleagues. Invite HR leaders in your organization to participate. This will help them learn more about the skills and capabilities that veterans bring with them to the civilian workplace.

Why Join an Affinity Group?

Many larger companies have affinity groups for different purposes. Don't hesitate to join the veterans' affinity group if one exists at your new civilian organization. If a veterans' affinity group doesn't exist, you can find steps on how to start one later in this chapter. Here are some benefits of participating in an affinity group:

- **Connect with other veterans.** It can be hard to know who in your organization has prior military service. It's not something that the HR department often tracks. An affinity group can provide a place to meet and form relationships with people who share your military experiences. This group will be more likely to understand your challenges and they might be able to offer tips based on how things have worked for them.

- **Find mentors.** It's easy to see how your network would expand by engaging with an affinity group. The common bond with the group will be your former military service, but there will be people in the group that come from all different backgrounds and positions in the organization.

- **Learn new things.** Again, you'll be given the opportunity to interact with people with different job titles and different responsibilities than your own. You can learn all about what other departments at the organization do, plus you can see different leadership styles in action.

- **Find new opportunities.** Affinity groups often host special training sessions or go on "field trips" that would expand both your knowledge and your exposure. Plus, you might have the opportunity to learn and show new skills. For example, maybe you'll agree to speak at a new member meeting where people can see your public speaking skills which you don't normally show in your regular job.

- **Make changes**. An affinity group can help the organization improve its veteran recruiting and retention. Maybe you'll volunteer to do job fairs or speak at a military conference. Or you could help the HR department track the careers of former military personnel. Or you can plan celebrations to recognize current members of the National Guard and Reserves. Any of these things will make a difference for both the organization and the veterans who work there.

How to Start an Affinity Group

If your organization does not have a veterans' affinity group, you can start one. All you really need is an interested group of people, a clear goal, and enthusiastic support. Here are some steps to consider as you work on setting up the group.

1. **Draft a mission statement.** The charter in the appendix of this book has a suggested mission statement but you can draft one that better captures what you want the group to do. (See Point #3 in this list for more about charters.) Maybe you want the group to really focus on recruiting more veterans into the organization so that should be reflected in your mission statement. Or maybe you simply want a social experience that gathers veterans each month to talk about their issues. By capturing the purpose of the group in clear, concise statements, you will make it easier to promote your group.

2. **Decide what resources you want.** Try to picture a few activities and make some estimates about how much money you would like the organization to provide to sponsor those activities. Start simple so you can follow through with the plans—and it'll be an easier "Yes" if the budget is reasonable. Be sure to think about where you want the group to meet. Maybe

it's easier to use workspace and your sponsor could help you find available space. Some groups meet at a coffee shop or have a potluck at someone's house to make things more casual and personal.

3. **Create a charter.** A charter is a written document created to provide direction for the affinity group. The group charter should provide a clear and simple mission that everyone in the group supports. The charter can also be a guide for any activity considered or pursued by the group. The appendix in this book provides a sample that can get you started on creating a charter for a new veterans' affinity group—or you can use the sample to update an existing group's charter with new ideas.

4. **Find your allies.** Who do you already know that might be interested in joining the group? Who could help you contact the veterans in your organization? Be sure to find a leader or a manager that would be willing to sponsor or promote your group to the organization, especially to the leaders who would approve and fund it.

5. **Promote the affinity group.** If there are a few veterans in your workplace who are already interested, that makes things easy. But if you're not sure, start developing communications and connections that will generate interest. Think about what would appeal to both potential members and the organizational leaders that will be approving your plans. Be prepared for push-back from leaders who might just not "see the point." While veterans will likely get natural support, some types of affinity groups struggle to convince leaders that their experiences are any different from the general population.

6. **Structure your meetings.** Review your mission statement to help guide you on what your meetings will look like. Will it have a formal process or be more of a roundtable discussion? Will there be a presentation, or just open conversations? Do you need to do any

planning for future events? People—particularly military people, as you know—like to rely on how the group will work and how things will be run, so it's good to establish the structure early.

7. **Assign roles.** Every group needs a leadership structure, but it's okay if the affinity group has a small group leading the way. The charter in this book's appendix has more information about the types of roles that are helpful in running the group, including suggested committees. Also, the next section, Roles in an Affinity Group, will help you select people that would be best in each role.

8. **Remember that it will take time.** You know you'll need to set aside time to organize, promote, and even hold the meetings. Be sure to share the responsibilities so you don't get burned out before it even gets off the ground. Also, you might have broader ideas where you really want to affect change in the organization. When it comes to these concepts, things rarely happen quickly. Recognize that goals that are bold and ambitious are wonderful, but you need to be patient to achieve them.

Roles in an Affinity Group

An affinity group should have a defined leadership team to help guide the group and make sure they stay on task. It also helps to spread the responsibilities among the group so one person doesn't end up doing all the work.

ROLE	COMMON RESPONSIBILITIES
Sponsor	• Act as a champion for the group • Ensure the affinity group is operating autonomously with continued organizational support • Share information about the group's activities with organizational leadership • Urge leaders of the affinity group to keep innovating to meet the needs of its members • Encourage attendance (by members and organizational leadership) at key events • Offer advice to the group's leadership that helps the group stay on track with the organization's direction
Chair	• Lead and oversee the group • Run the meetings and other events • Ensure the group charter is supported and regularly updated • Accompany sponsor to meet with leaders in the organization to explain what the group is doing and to make any funding requests

Vice-Chair	• Assist or act if the Chair is not available • Help ensure that the charter is followed • Meet with committee chairs to answer questions and provide guidance • Draft and send communications to all group members and potential members • Learn about the group and the organizational leadership to prepare for role as the Chair
Organizational Liaison	• Provide support and information to the sponsor to help the sponsor promote and advocate for the group • Act as the contact point for all questions about the affinity group • Collaborate and communicate with the community for events or public service opportunities
Treasurer	• Support the administrative functions of the group • Keep membership lists, contact information, and other records up-to-date • Prepare monthly activity and budget reports as required by the group, the sponsor, and the organization • Prepare requests for annual budget with supporting documentation

Other Ideas for Your Veterans' Affinity Group

Whether you joined an existing group, or you are starting a new veterans' affinity group, you might need more ideas for types of activities the group can do. As you can see, there are many options that go beyond simply talking about shared experiences. The group has the opportunity to truly dive into making an organizational impact. This is where you can really make a difference for current and future employees of the organization that have served in the military.

The Veterans Administration understands how veterans' affinity groups can make a difference in the civilian workplace. They developed a handout in their Veterans Employment Toolkit that provides definitions for veterans' affinity groups, along with suggestions on how the group can impact an organization.

- Hold social activities and include family members where possible.

- Celebrate holiday remembrances (such as Veterans Day) inside and outside the organization.

- Create a communication platform (preferably online) so members know about meetings, events, and other ways to get involved. Allow for open discussions among members using this communication platform.

- Maintain an active social media presence to improve member communications, provide visibility to organizational leaders, and create community support for members.

- Organize career development workshops and training.

- Invite key leaders to help members grow and advance within the organization.

- Discuss leadership in the civilian workplace compared to military experiences and training.

- Assist with veteran recruiting which may include being the organizational representative at job fairs and college recruiting events.

- Attend networking events to help your organization connect with veteran candidates.

- Act as an internal focus group for the organization, giving the veterans' perspective on organizational changes or even external product or service reviews.

- Give advice to human resources and management on improving policies and programs.

- Connect new group members with mentors who are veterans and have been with the organization for a long time.

- Offer training to volunteer mentors within the group so the mentors can improve their skills and create a positive experience for their mentee.

- Maintain a list of veteran services within the organization, and the steps to seeking assistance.

- Create a list of community resources and support systems that veterans at the organization might need. Include resources for spouses and family members.

11

UNDERSTANDING CIVILIAN PAY AND BENEFITS

You will be excited when you make it to the final stages of the hiring process and receive an offer for a job that aligns with your values. Still, there are several important considerations before you accept. This chapter will help you understand how pay and benefits work in civilian organizations. Every employer is going to be a little different in how they handle these issues, but this information will at least help you ask questions about your pay and benefits package.

When you examine a job offer, you need to understand the total compensation package. Total compensation is more than just pay—it's everything of value that an employer provides in exchange for the work you do. Looking at the total compensation package is important for several reasons. First, benefits usually help you pay for things you may need, like medical or dental care. Without such coverage, you may not even be able to afford to get medical care. You usually get better rates by being part of employer medical or life insurance plans than you get if you purchased a policy independently.

Second, some benefits can help you maintain a healthy work–life balance. Some organizations understand that it is challenging for employees to balance their job duties with things that need to happen at home. Many benefit packages are designed to help relieve this stress. For example, an organization may allow you to work from home for a certain number of days each week. Avoiding a long commute every day might really help make the difference in having a life that meets your personal vision. Another example is paid time off for volunteer activities. Some companies even arrange group volunteer days during the week where everyone works together for a community project while getting paid their regular wages. Even if the pay is slightly lower than what you wanted, having some of these benefits might make you really consider accepting an offer of employment. Again, making strong social bonds with other people like you both inside and outside of work will increase the likelihood that you'll still be in the same job several years later.

Third, a strong total compensation package can help you prepare for the future. Be sure to ask about what kind of training or conferences that the company would be able to offer you. Tuition assistance is also a popular benefit which you could use to get a degree or a certification. All these things could eventually lead to promotions or higher wages. Plus, a good 401(k) plan with a company match could help you prepare for eventual retirement and make your future more secure.

If you haven't already, you should log into your military payroll system and request and download a copy of your Personal Statement of Military Compensation. If your branch of service uses the MyPay system through DFAS, you can access your Personal Statement of Military Compensation and download it on to your computer. Your personal statement lists all the benefits you are receiving on active duty and paints a better picture of what you're really receiving from the federal government for your service. This is your total compensation package. The statement lists your "direct compensation," which is the actual pay you're receiving each month. It also lists "indirect compensation," which are the benefits you receive in addition to your pay.

As an example, you don't have to pay federal taxes on your BAH and BAS. Not having to pay taxes on that income means you're going to have access to more money each month based on that tax savings. The Servicemembers Group Life Insurance that you have is another type of indirect compensation. Your premiums are lower than they would be if you were a civilian and tried to purchase a similar life insurance policy. You can use your personal statement as a guide to help you negotiate your civilian job because it will help you understand the total compensation you've actually been receiving as a U.S. service member.

Pay

Most civilian organizations will offer you a job using a formal offer letter. The letter should include information about how you will be paid. It will likely tell you if you will be paid on an hourly or salaried basis, how often you get paychecks, and if you will be eligible for commission or bonus payments. In most cases, the listed pay will be what you make before taxes, so take-home pay may be very different than what is stated in the offer. If you need help in determining how much you will actually be bringing home each paycheck, ask the HR representative to help you with the calculations.

- **Hourly pay** is the rate that you make for each hour that you work. Hourly employees must be paid time and a half for any hours beyond 40 during a work week.

- **Salaried employees** receive a fixed wage, and they don't get paid for working extra hours. A salary is usually quoted as an annual wage, but sometimes offer letters will show monthly amounts as well.

The Fair Labor Standards Act determines whether a position is paid on an hourly or salaried basis.

Salary Ranges

Most employers decide how much to pay employees by establishing a salary range. A salary range is the amount that the organization has determined is appropriate to pay a specific position. The range usually lists a minimum and maximum pay amount, as well as a mid-point so you know how you compare to other people in the range. For example, a pay range might have a minimum salary of $32,000 and a maximum pay of $45,000. This means the employer can offer you any number between those two salary levels for your position. To establish salary ranges, the organization considers the following:

- **Data**. Employers share their pay rates for similar positions with market researchers who publish studies that show market pay rates for a wide variety of jobs.

- **Market**. Pay levels are impacted by market factors like how many jobs are available, and the number of available candidates.

- **Internal Equity**. Some organizations look at the relationship between different jobs in their company and compare which jobs are more important to the company and/or more difficult to perform.

- **Budget**. A company will have to determine the budget they have available for paying each person.

Employers typically have flexibility when it comes to how much to pay a new employee. A highly qualified and experienced candidate can expect a job offer that's at the higher end of the salary range, while a candidate who is brand new to the workforce or who does not have much experience in the actual job will likely be offered a salary closer to the minimum. Your place in a salary range depends on the following aspects:

- **Experience.** The length of time you have worked in a related area or industry affects how much you will be paid.

- **Results**: If you can show that you were very valuable in your military role, you may often receive higher offers.

- **Industry:** Some industries, like education and union manufacturing, often have strict salary steps based on how long you work in each role.

- **The job market**: If it's difficult to find employees in your field or with your skills, you are more likely to receive offers in the upper level of the range.

- **Skillset:** Certain skills or certifications may be in higher demand and can get higher pay. That's why it's so important to be able to translate your military experience into civilian language.

- **Company size:** Larger organizations with more formal HR structures are more likely to have set salary ranges, while small organizations might have more flexibility in making salary offers.

Benefits

Benefits are an important part of your total pay package and you should make sure you understand what an organization offers before you accept an employment offer. In most cases, employers pay for a portion of your benefits, and some employers pay for most or all of them. How much your employer expects you to contribute toward your benefits may change from year to year as benefit prices change.

Medical Coverage

On active duty, you just needed to schedule an appointment with your military treatment facility to receive health care. If you lived a certain distance from a military treatment facility, you were able to use your Tricare medical insurance to receive medical care that was away from your camp, post or station. On your Leave and Earnings Statement, you can see how much your Tricare insurance costs you each month. Unless you are retiring from active duty, you will lose access to your Tricare coverage when you leave service.

Medical insurance helps cover the high cost of medical care. You will need to spend some time learning about the medical insurance plans offered by your company to understand how the coverage works.

TYPE OF PLAN	HOW IT WORKS	WHO MIGHT BENEFIT
Health Maintenance Organization (HMO)	You can only use medical providers who work for or contract with the HMO. If you use providers that aren't "in the network," the charges usually aren't covered except in an emergency.	People who don't use medical services very much or only see a few doctors.
Preferred Provider Organization (PPO)	You pay less if you use providers in the plan's network, but you can see providers outside the network. You don't need a referral if you want to see a specialist, such as an OB/GYN.	People who want more freedom to direct their own care.
Point-of-Service (POS)	You pay less if you use providers in the plan's network, but you can see providers outside the network. If you want to see a specialist, you must get a referral from your Primary Care Physician.	People who have a wide variety of medical needs and would benefit from having that care coordinated by a Primary Care doctor.

Catastrophic Plan	This plan offers coverage for emergencies and preventive care, and typically comes with low monthly premiums. There may be certain age requirements to enroll in the coverage (such as being under the age of thirty).	People who rarely seek medical care but need protection in case of an emergency.
High Deductible Health Plan	This plan has a higher deductible* than most plans but it often has lower monthly premiums. Preventive care is usually covered at 100% if you use an in-network provider. Usually offered with a Health Savings Account (see below).	People who can afford to pay the deductible, and want lower premiums. Or people who want access to the tax savings offered by a Health Savings Account.

In a medical insurance plan, a deductible is the amount of money you have to pay for medical services before the insurance starts paying expenses. For example, if your plan has a $1,000 deductible, then you need to pay for $1,000 of medical expenses before the plan starts paying for your medical care. The deductible usually starts over each calendar year.

Health Savings Account

If you enroll in a qualified High Deductible Health Plan, you may be able to open a Health Savings Account. Health Savings Accounts (HSAs) are like personal savings accounts, but you use the money in them to pay for health care expenses. You—not your employer or insurance company—own and control the money in your HSA.

One reason people are interested in HSAs is that the money you deposit into the account is not taxed. Sometimes, employers will also deposit money into the HSA and that is not taxable income for you either. Some HSAs pay interest on the money in your account or invest the money in mutual funds. Any earnings from an HSA are also tax-free. Each year, the Internal Revenue Service announces how much you will be allowed to deposit into your HSA.

An HSA may not be right for everyone, but if you're pretty healthy and you want to set aside tax-free savings for future health care expenses, an HSA may be an attractive choice. If you're near retirement, an HSA may make sense because the money can be used to offset the costs of medical care after retirement. On the other hand, if you think you might need expensive medical care in the next year and you're concerned about having to meet a high deductible, an HSA with the high deductible health plan might not be your best option.

Dental Coverage

Dental coverage is insurance that pays for treatment by a dentist. Most employers offer dental coverage, but you will likely have to pay premiums for the coverage out of your paycheck. Usually, dental insurance benefits pay for annual examinations and X-rays as well as preventive dental treatment. If you need to have a filling or other repair work on your teeth, the insurance may pay for part of those expenses. Dental insurance usually covers orthodontic work, but there are almost always limits on how much they will pay. Some plans require that you use certain dentists, so you'll want to check that out before you make an appointment for dental services.

Vision Coverage

You should figure out if the medical plan that you choose covers annual routine eye exams—many have that as part of the medical preventive care benefits. Plus, some employers offer separate vision insurance but—like dental coverage—you will likely have to pay premiums for the coverage out of your paycheck. Most vision insurance plans allow you to get an annual eye exam for free and may pay for contacts or glasses up to a certain dollar amount. Some plans offer discounts on elective vision correction surgery, like Lasik. Whether you should buy vision insurance depends on how often you visit the eye doctor, whether you wear corrective lenses, and many other factors. Take time and estimate the costs you expect to have for vision care each year and compare those to what the insurance costs and offers. You may find out that it is cheaper for you not to buy the insurance and to pay for your vision expenses on your own.

Flexible Spending Accounts

If you have medical coverage through your civilian employer, you can use a Flexible Spending Account (FSA) to pay for copayments, deductibles, prescription drug expenses, and some other health care costs. An FSA is a special account where you deposit money to use to pay for certain out-of-pocket health care costs. The major advantage of using an FSA is that you don't pay taxes on the money you deposit into the account. Most employers automatically deduct the amount you choose right from your paycheck—before taxes are withheld—and deposit that money for you into your FSA. There are a few things that are important to understand about FSAs.

- Each year, the Internal Revenue Service announces how much you will be allowed to deposit into your FSA.

- You must use the money in your FSA by the end of the calendar year or you may lose that money. Some employers allow for grace periods or some amounts that can be rolled over. You should ask questions about that if you are interested in setting aside money in an FSA.

- It's pretty easy to get reimbursed from most FSAs. Many have online tools where you can submit receipts from your eligible expenses and they transfer money directly into your regular bank account. Some even have a debit card that allows you to pay for eligible expenses directly from the FSA.

Some employers also offer another type of FSA called a dependent-care flexible spending account. It works the same as a healthcare FSA but with the dependent-care FSA, you use the money to pay for childcare expenses for children age twelve and under, or for the care of qualifying adults who cannot care for themselves. Again, the major advantage of using an FSA is that you don't pay taxes on the money you deposit into the account.

Life Insurance

On active duty, you have the ability to receive life insurance at a significant discount through the Servicemembers Group Life Insurance plan. That insurance is provided by a private vendor of the federal government, and the premiums for that insurance have been deducted each month from your paycheck. If you look at one of your Leave and Earnings Statements, you can see how much that insurance costs you every month. If a triggering event would have occurred, the vendor would have paid that life insurance benefit to whomever you had listed as the beneficiary on your life insurance policy. The payments would not have been paid from the federal government.

Once you leave active duty, you will lose access to your Servicemembers Group Life Insurance. You will be able to obtain life insurance through another discounted program called the Veterans' Group Life Insurance (VGLI) program. In a nutshell, you will need to apply for VGLI coverage within 120 days of leaving the military and if you secure a policy within 240 days of leaving service, you will not have to receive a physical to be covered. There are other civilian insurance companies that will offer you comparable life insurance coverage once you leave active duty. Take a little time and research whether it makes sense for you to pay for the VGLI insurance or if it's cheaper to get the same level of insurance through another carrier for a smaller monthly premium.

Many employers pay for a certain amount of life insurance coverage for every employee. If you die, life insurance provides money for a beneficiary, usually a family member. You may have a chance to buy additional life insurance coverage through your employer where the company takes deductions out of your paycheck to pay for the coverage.

Disability Insurance

If you were injured while serving on active duty, all you had to do was go to the medical treatment facility or medical provider and tell your supervisor that you were injured. You were able to stay at home for an indefinite period to recuperate and still receive your full pay and benefits every month. In the civilian world, you will need to secure a special type of insurance called disability insurance to pay all or some of your pay and living expenses if you're unable to work due to a medical condition.

The Social Security Administration estimates that one in four twenty-year-olds will experience a disability for ninety days or more before they reach sixty-seven years of age. Disability insurance pays you a portion of your income if you become sick or injured and are unable to work. Keep in mind that if your organization does not offer paid maternity leave, this insurance is usually used to pay for time away from work after having a baby. There are generally two types of disability coverage offered by employers:

- **Short-term disability (STD).** These benefits are designed to replace your income for shorter periods away from work. They are typically used for a few months until you can get back to work, and almost never more than a year.

- **Long-term disability (LTD).** These benefits are designed to last for many years—up to age 65 if needed—replacing around 40%–60% of your income if something happens and you can no longer work.

Your total compensation package may include some levels of STD or LTD at no cost to you, and you may be able to purchase additional coverage with deductions from your paycheck. You may also be allowed to choose if you want to have your disability benefit payments taxable or not, which affects the tax status of how your premiums are deducted from your paycheck.

Retirement Plans

Before 2020, active-duty personnel had to serve for twenty years on active duty to receive a pension, which is called a defined benefit plan in the civilian world. The twenty-year pension paid a benefit that was calculated as a percentage of the service member's base pay based on total years of service. A service member who received $3,000 base pay each month and had 20 years of service would receive $1,500/month, which was calculated as a percentage of base pay (2.5 ×20). After 2020, the Department of Defense established the Blended Retirement System (BRS) which pays a pension that is calculated at a lesser rate using 2.0 as the multiplier instead of 2.5. So a service member with $3,000 in base pay each month would only receive $1,200 each month after they retire under the BRS system.

The BRS added an additional benefit to help service members build their retirement nest egg and be able to take it with them if they didn't want to do twenty years. With BRS, the federal government will match a certain portion of the service member's deposits to their Thrift Savings Plan, which is called a defined contribution plan in the civilian world. If you have money invested in a Thrift Savings Plan, you will be able to take that retirement savings with you when you leave active duty.

The most common type of retirement savings plans that employers offer is a 401(k) plan, which is similar to the federal government's Thrift Savings Plan. The catchy name comes from the section of the tax code—specifically subsection 401(k)—that created this type of plan. If you choose to participate in your company 401(k) plan, you contribute money to an individual account by signing up for automatic deductions from your paycheck. With most 401(k) plans, these automatic deductions are made before taxes are calculated on your pay. This means that you don't pay taxes on the money you contribute to the plan. Each year, the Internal Revenue Service announces how much you will be allowed to contribute to your 401(k) plan account.

Many employers offer to match employee contributions, either dollar for dollar or fifty cents to the dollar, up to a set limit. For example, say you make $40,000 a year and your organization offers a 401(k) match of 50% up to the first 6% you contribute. If you contribute 6% of your annual pay ($2,400), your employer would contribute an additional $1,200 to your 401(k) plan. Be sure to ask if the matching contributions are yours immediately or if they "vest" over time. Some employers use a vesting schedule where you gradually take ownership of those matching contributions over several years to encourage you to stay with the organization. These vesting rules encourage employees to stay with an organization longer so they can maximize their retirement benefits.

You will usually have several investment options in your 401(k) plan such as different mutual funds or index funds. You get to decide how much of your 401(k) balance to invest in different funds. For example, you could choose to put 70% of your contributions in an international mutual fund, and 30% in a bond index fund. Target Date funds are popular too. A Target Date fund invests your savings in a mix of stocks and bonds that is determined by your current age and your "target" date for retirement. Investing options available in company 401(k) plans vary widely. You should consider consulting with a financial adviser to help you figure out the best investing strategy for you.

There are a few other types of retirement plans that you might see in a civilian organization. They are all designed to help you set aside money to be used in retirement. Here are a few of them with a quick definition for each one:

- **Profit Sharing Plan**. Gives you a share of the profits of the company, usually based on quarterly or annual earnings.

- **Simplified Employee Pension (SEP) IRA**. Available to sole proprietors, partnerships, and corporations. Only your employer can make contributions to this type of plan but you manage the investment decisions for the money.

- **Employee Stock Ownership Plan (ESOP)**. Enables you to own part of the company you work for. You would receive the value of your shares from a trust when you retire.

- **403(b) Plan.** Very similar to a 401(k) plan and is usually used in the education or non-profit industries.

- **457 Plan**. Similar to a 401(k) plan and is generally seen in the government or non-profit sector. Allows you to withdraw funds as soon as you leave the organization, rather than having to wait until age 59 ½, like most retirement plans.

- **Cash-balance Plan.** A twist on the traditional pension plan where you have an individual account set up on your behalf. When you retire, you can decide if you take your savings as a lump sum or as a lifetime annuity.

Paid Time Off

In the military, you received 2.5 days of annual leave each month, which was in addition to your ability to receive passes and take benefit of training holidays, which usually were connected to federal holidays. Although the rules for carrying over leave balances have changed from time-to-time, you generally had to "use or lose" your annual leave if you kept it for longer than a year. Maternity leave, paternity leave, transition leave, and house hunting leave are other forms of paid time off.

The amount of paid time off you get each year will vary widely from company to company. There isn't a federal statute or regulation that requires employers to even offer this benefit. The federal Fair Labor Standards Act doesn't require payment for time not worked. However, each state has laws about paid time off that will impact how employers manage their policies.

Paid time off is definitely one of the things you should look at very closely when you consider what kind of job to accept in this next phase of your life. Again, examine your top five values to determine how important this is to you and see if your job offer has the right program to meet your needs. Sometimes, you can even negotiate more or different paid time off options if an organization is willing to make exceptions to its policies. Here are some questions to help you better understand how paid time off works at your potential employer:

- Do you have a traditional vacation plus sick time policy or do you use a combined paid time off program?

- Will I start accruing vacation days right away or is there a waiting period?

- How many days or hours of vacation do I earn each month?

- Is paid time off tracked by each calendar year or does it work with my hire/anniversary date?

- How many years of service do I need before I get additional vacation days?

- Can I take paid time off in smaller amounts, or do I have to take a full day off?

- Can I roll over any unused time off? Is there a cap on how much I can roll over?

- Are there any personal days or floating holidays? What are the rules around how these can be used?

Employee Assistance Programs

An employee assistance program (EAP) is a benefit provided by a company to help employees address issues that could impact their life and their work. EAPs are usually offered to employees at little or no cost. The range of services offered by an EAP depends on the contract that the employer selects. Some organizations offer free visits with a certified therapist, along with smoking cessation or weight loss programs. A bigger EAP benefit might include access to wellness classes, financial counseling, legal assistance, or elder care referral services.

One thing to consider is that EAP services can be really helpful in managing career transitions. You should be eligible for EAP services as soon as you are hired at a company so think about reaching out right away to get the support you need to smoothly settle into your new responsibilities and new organization.

Other Benefits

When it comes to benefits and perks, some companies have started offering some unique things to differentiate themselves from other employers. They are trying to attract top talent and appeal to a multi-generational workforce. Be on the lookout for some of these offerings:

- Student Loan Repayment Plans
- Discounts on travel and ride-sharing
- Discounts on cell phone or Wi-Fi plans
- Pet insurance
- Long-term care insurance
- Restaurant vouchers
- Employee referral programs
- Financial literacy classes

- Complimentary parking
- On-site gyms or gym membership reimbursement
- Biometric screenings
- Adoption assistance
- Charitable contributions
- Flexible schedules like four-day workweeks
- Technology reimbursement for home office

Enrolling in Benefits: Open Enrolment

When you first start working for a civilian employer, you will be guided through the process of how to enroll in the company benefits. With most types of benefits, once you make a choice, you are committed to that option for an entire year with only a few exceptions. You will be unable to change your benefit choices until the open enrollment period or if you have a "qualifying event" like a marriage or birth of a child.

Open enrollment is a period of time each year when you can sign up for benefits or you can change your plan choices. The open enrollment period is also an opportunity to disenroll if you no longer want the coverage. During this period, you will likely be asked to review your benefit choices for medical, dental, and vision coverage, as well as life insurance, disability insurance and Flexible Spending Accounts. Most organizations have an open enrollment period that lasts a few weeks, typically at the end of the year. Watch for communications about open enrollment so you don't miss it and accidentally miss out on getting coverage for a benefit that you want or need.

Evaluating the Total Compensation Package

Of course, pay is important when you are offered a job. However, it's important to evaluate the entire total compensation package before you decide to accept the role. Here are some questions to consider when evaluating a job offer:

What's most important to you?

Revisit your Values Exercise to see if any of your top five values could be impacted by the total compensation package. For example, if Family is on your list, you might want to take a close look at the time off benefits, or the work-from-home options. Or maybe Security made the list, so base pay and a strong retirement plan might be most important to you. As you begin the job search, know which parts of the total compensation package are most important to you. If there's something missing when you get a job offer, talk to the organization about why a particular benefit is important to you.

How should you compare your military pay and benefits to an offer from a civilian organization?

The best place to start is to go back to your Personal Statement of Military Compensation. You will see that it lists additional benefits like having access to free wills and powers of attorney, notary services, free tax advice, and many other benefits. Whether you used those additional benefits or not, those additional benefits will cost you real money when you leave active duty. You will want to review your personal statement before your job interview and then read it again after you have received a job offer. This will enable you to compare your total compensation that you had on active duty and see how that measures up to what's in your job offer.

What details do you need?

You've already answered what's most important to you when you are look-ing for a role in a civilian organization. Once you have a job offer, it will be important to take a deeper dive into the benefits that are most important to you. As discussed in this chapter, the offerings for medical insurance vary greatly. You'll want to understand how the medical services you use the most are covered. For example, if your family is taking prescription medicine, how much will you have to pay for those drugs? Ask for summaries of the key programs, or ask for actual policy documents if you have the time to read them.

What are the eligibility rules for each benefit?

Some benefit programs are open only to employees who have been with the company for a certain period of time. For example, you might not be able to receive the company match into your 401(k) plan until you work for one year. Or a tuition reimbursement benefit might require a boss's approval. While some of the rules are guided by written plan documents or insurance regulations, it's possible for you to negotiate in some areas. You might be currently working on a certification program (that may have been listed as one of your Learning Goals). Consider requesting that your job offer include a part indicating how the company will pay for the rest of the fees for the certification program—or you could have the organization provide time off to study that does not take away any days from your Paid Time Off package.

Questions to Ask about Total Compensation

During the interviews, you may have the opportunity to ask questions of a Human Resources or Benefits representative. You can ask anything to clarify your understanding of how any of the benefits work. Here are some suggestions for things you might not have considered asking:

- How are pay increases determined? When does that happen?
- How much will be deducted from my paycheck for benefits like medical or dental insurance?
- Is my domestic partner eligible for benefits?
- What does the organization do to promote wellness? Are there discounts or reimbursements for wellness services?

- Am I allowed to choose my own investments for my 401(k) plan savings?

- Do I have to earn my Paid Time Off, or is it just given to me in one block at the beginning of each year?

- Do you have a performance review process? Is it connected to pay?

- What training and development programs will I be able to access?

- What help is available so I can make good choices about what benefits are right for me and my family?

- Do you have a Veterans Affinity Group?

You don't want to be caught off guard after you start your new job because you didn't ask enough questions about the total compensation package. So don't be embarrassed to ask for more information.

12

OUTPROCESSING: NOBODY'S GOING TO THROW YOU A PARADE

There's a lot of excitement that accompanies enlisting in the U.S. armed forces or receiving your commission. Your life in the military likely started with significant discussions with important family members as you weighed options about which branch of service you wanted to join. Recruiters helped you select your military operational specialty and the timing to attend basic training and advanced training. You had to pass an incredibly detailed physical at a Military Entrance Processing Station (MEPS) and sign a good deal of paperwork. All that work and process culminated in you standing in a ceremony at MEPS or with a recruiter, or at your commissioning ceremony where you were surrounded by your closest friends and family as you raised your right hand and swore to protect and defend the United States against all enemies, foreign and domestic. The ceremony served as a reminder that what you were about to do was important. People took pictures and maybe even got a little teary-eyed that you were about to "ship off" to basic, your officer's basic course, ROTC, or an academy.

In addition to your friends and family, there was an entire team of military recruiters who were experts in making sure that you signed all the paperwork correctly, passed your physical, and made it to your first military training course. The Department of Defense invested a good deal of money and resources to get you to that point—getting ready to leave for your first school or duty assignment. Again, the system is set-up to recruit and enlist quality service members and make sure they make it to their first duty assignment. From there, cadres of officers and non-commissioned officers train and guide service members through the military system to make sure that the DoD got the most out of everyone. You were an investment in national diplomacy and national security.

It will not be like that when you leave service. You won't experience any of the pomp and ceremony that surrounded your enlistment or commissioning. That's because the DoD had a significant interest in making sure you made it through your basic training and other courses so you could serve the rest of your commitment and contribute to your unit, branch, and within the DoD apparatus. The DoD does not have the same level of interest in making sure you smoothly integrate into society as you secure your first civilian job and start building your new life.

There will also be less people involved in helping you outprocess from active duty. The outprocessing team will focus on making sure you use all your leave or get paid for what leave you don't use. They will make sure your DD-214 properly lists all your awards, your years of service, and characterization of discharge. They will track that you've turned in all your military gear, and if you haven't, they will assess charges for the gear you were unable to turn-in before you left service. Those charges will be either taken out of your last pay or from your IRS tax return depending on various conditions. Your outprocessing team will be subject matter experts in every way to make sure all the paperwork is signed before you leave active duty. Your retirement counselor will talk about military pay, healthcare coverage, disability benefits, and other types of insurance and other benefits that you may be entitled to receive when you leave service. But there will be no parade.

Medical Outprocessing

When you first came onto active duty, one of the first things you did was endure a pretty rigorous military entrance physical at a Military Entrance Processing Station (MEPS). The Department of Defense conducts entrance physicals for two reasons: to make sure you meet the physical standards for service and to identify a baseline for any disability benefits you may receive when you leave active service.

When you leave service, you will go through another intensive physical before you leave. This is the physical that will show the Veterans Administration whether you may qualify for VA benefits. Your branch of service will give the VA electronic access to your military medical records to review your VA disability claim. Service members have options in how they file their VA claims. They can file their own claim with the VA. They can hire a law firm to help with the claim and agree to pay a fee to the law firm. Or they can use free services provided by their state's Department of Military and Veteran Affairs or with a Veteran Service Officer (VSO) with organizations like AMVETS, the American Legion, and the Veterans of Foreign Wars. VSOs have been trained by the VA and are certified by the VA to file claims on a veteran's behalf. Veterans do not have to be members of those organizations to ask for help in filing a claim, but they should keep in mind that all VSOs are not the same. You will want to find one that is the best fit for you. Here are a couple tips for your final medical outprocessing:

- **Obtain records of civilian provider care.** If you've been treated by civilian providers during service, make sure you obtain a copy of all your treatment to include as part of your VA claim. The DoD does not keep copies of those records and the VA won't have access to them unless you provide them in support of your VA claim.

- **Be honest.** This is the time to be completely honest with how you are doing physically and mentally. If you've been struggling with falling asleep or have anger management issues, make sure to tell your provider. Make sure your outprocessing physician documents each diagnosis in your official record.

- **Do your research.** It'll be helpful if you spend some time researching the most common VA disability claims. There are a lot of great YouTube videos on common claims. Watch a couple videos and see if you have experienced any common ailments that warrant documenting.

- **PTS and PTSD.** Many veterans spent their entire career lying about their struggles with PTS and PTSD. They worry that if they went to counseling or admitted they get depressed, they will be overlooked for promotions or given bad assignments. Those worries are over. Be completely honest with your physicians when you talk about any mental health issues you've experienced during your time in uniform.

- **Don't be too proud.** Many veterans simply don't file VA claims because they don't think they should be paid for what happened to them during service or they don't want to see themselves as a "disabled veteran." The VA system is set up to compensate you and your family for your physical and mental health injuries. Take a deep breath and start putting together your records for your VA disability claim.

- **Compile your military records.** If you've deployed or have been treated at your basic training site or by another branch of service, you should assume that those records are not in your electronic medical files. Spend some time with your military medical provider and look at your file before you leave service. If you have missing records, hunt them down and make sure they make it into your official file.

Before Going to Outprocessing

During your outprocessing, you will be meeting mostly with GS civilians who will be walking you through all the different stages of outprocessing. To make sure the outprocessing team gets everything right on your paperwork, pay, and benefits, you will want to spend some time preparing.

- **Designate an outprocessing notebook.** You can pick a notebook, a binder, or any filing system, but just keep all your papers and your notes together. You will be given a lot of information during your outprocessing and it's easy to forget all the bits and pieces of the information after you leave their office. Plus, you may have random outprocessing questions at any point in your day so keep your note-taking system close to make sure all your information is together.

- **Gather all records.** Bring any records you think will be able to help them get things right. Keep in mind that the outprocessing team can only see records that are in your electronic files. This is especially important if you have recently received an award because there's a chance the award documentation will not have found its way into your electronic file by the day of your outprocessing.

- **Make copies of records.** Create two copies of all the documents you plan to bring: one copy will go to the processing clerks and the second copy is yours to reference as you go through the different outprocessing stations.

Common Record Challenges

Bring copies of anything recent that has happened in your military career. If your command wasn't able to upload a recent award into your official electronic file, the outprocessing team may not be able to see it and they won't be able to record it on your final DD-214. If you've recently completed a military school, bring your school's graduation paperwork with you. Bring copies of all your DD-214s to receive full credit for any time you spent on active duty during earlier service, a prior deployment, or service with another branch of service. Don't assume that your records from your previous service have found their way into your current electronic file.

- **Bring divorce judgments.** If you've gone through a divorce since serving on active duty, you will need a copy of your final judgment of divorce and child support orders (if applicable). These documents are necessary to establish the percentage of pay your former spouse may be entitled to receive and to identify whether your former spouse is entitled to any portion of your survivor benefit annuity. You may be tempted not to bring these documents with you, but that can cause significant problems down the road. If you are obligated to give your former spouse a percentage of your retirement pay and don't disclose it during your outprocessing, you run the risk of having your former spouse bringing you back into the court system to enforce the prior judgment of divorce. Lawyer fees can be expensive, and it's not uncommon for judges to punish service members who knowingly fail to disclose a preexisting obligation for payment. You're much better off disclosing any spousal support obligations during your outprocessing and dealing with it head-on.

- **Meet with your supply office.** Although each branch of service uses different processes to handle missing equipment, the government will seek to recover money if their electronic systems are showing that you didn't turn something in before you leave service. Your supply office can review any issued equipment on record. Any gear that you haven't turned in will cost you during outprocessing. Take a paper copy of your final equipment receipt with you to address any discrepancies between what the system says and what your supply office says. If there are any pieces of military gear that you could not find, the government will deduct the value of those items from your final pay or from your retired pay.

Military Pay

If you're retiring, your outprocessing office will calculate a retirement pay estimate based on your years of service, rank, and other factors. That pay estimate will be sent through your retirement office to a branch in the Defense Finance and Accounting Service (DFAS) to perform the final calculations for your retired pay. Keep in mind that the estimates that you receive during your outprocessing are not necessarily the pay you will receive when you start collecting your retired pay. DFAS completes the final calculations in determining how much you will receive each month.

Your outprocessing office will go through several layers of approvals before they forward the pay estimate to DFAS. Once DFAS receives the pay request, DFAS will repeat the process. What's this mean to you? It's very likely that you will experience a "pay hiccup." Your active duty pay will stop once you leave active duty and your retirement pay won't be able to start until all the approvals have been issued and loaded into the payroll system. This can mean going without pay for several weeks. Plan ahead and work on setting aside some funding to cover up to one month of salary if there is a pay hiccup.

Good news: When you do receive your pay, it will include any pay for the pay gap. Bad news: you won't know how long the pay gap will last so make early plans to fill-in that financial gap. When you go through your outprocessing, make sure you ask how long your branch of service and DFAS typically takes to process the retirement pay request so you have an idea on how long you may go without pay. Write that information down in your outprocessing notebook so you remember this important information after you leave station.

Leave

You will have an opportunity to "cash in" your leave when you leave service. Your outprocessing counselor will talk to you about whether it makes sense for you to take your remaining leave or have it paid out. When the military pays you for your remaining leave, you will only receive your base pay for each day of leave you have on the books. As an example, if you have fifteen days of leave available and want the military to pay you for it, you will receive an additional pay on your next paycheck for half of your base pay for one month. That pay will not include payment for your housing allowance (BAH), food allowance (BAS) or for any other specialty pays.

To maximize the amount of money you can receive, work with your unit and your outprocessing office to allow you to take all of your leave before you leave service. This will take a little planning to make sure you have the time to take your leave before leaving service. You will want to build a leave plan to allow you to take any regular leave, terminal leave, and transition leave before you exit active duty. Take your signed leave forms with you when you go to outprocessing to make sure your version of your leave plan matches what the military thinks you can do with your remaining leave. Failing to do this might result in you sitting in the outprocessing office with leave on the books that you may not be able to use before your ETS happens. This could cost you hundreds of dollars. The best financial decision is always to use all your leave before you leave service. Even so, you will likely encounter other service members during your outprocessing who will hit their ETS date before they were able to use all their leave.

Survivor Benefit Plan and Life Insurance

The survivor benefit plan (SBP) is managed by a private entity that is not affiliated with the DoD. With the survivor benefit plan, you are purchasing an annuity that will provide up to 55% of your retirement pay to your spouse, your children, or a former spouse if you pass away while you are collecting your retired pay. Generally speaking, once you make this election during your outprocessing, you will be unable to change your mind once you start collecting your retired pay. While you're receiving retired pay, the DoD will deduct a monthly payment from your retirement check to pay for the annuity. Your outprocessing office will give you estimates of how much it will cost for you to purchase the SBP annuity, and they will need to know if you are electing to purchase the SBP before they can estimate your retired pay.

You do not have to take a SBP annuity that will pay the full 55% of your base pay to your former spouse or dependent. You can elect to receive lesser percentages of your pay, which will reduce the amount of the monthly premium that you will have to pay out of your retirement paycheck. If you do elect to have 55% of your base pay to be paid to your beneficiary, you will be charged a premium that is calculated at 6.5% of your base salary that you would be receiving during your retirement. For example, if your retirement pay is $2,000 per month and you elected the 55% SBP option, you would have to pay 6.5% of the $2,000 each month to pay for the SBP annuity, which is $130 per month.

Take note: If you were divorced at any time during your service, have a JAG officer or private attorney review your divorce documents to see whether your former spouse is entitled to any portion of your SBP. If they are, you will need to bring a copy of your divorce judgment to your outprocessing to make sure the retirement outprocessing team addresses your SBP payment requirements for your former spouse.

Should you take the full SBP annuity at 55% or a lesser amount? That depends. You may want to consider life insurance options to meet the needs of your personal situation. You will lose your Servicemembers Group Life

Insurance (SGLI) when you leave service. But you will be able to secure Veterans' Group Life Insurance (VGLI) once you separate. The VGLI premiums will be higher than they were when you had SGLI coverage while you were serving on active duty. One benefit of VGLI coverage is that you do not have to do a medical examination to be approved for a VGLI insurance policy. Other options for insurance coverage come from other veteran-friendly companies like the United Services Automobile Association (USAA). USAA typically offers the same level of term life insurance coverage that is offered with the VGLI coverage, and it usually costs a little less. Reach out to other insurance companies, like USAA, before you separate to see what life insurance options might be available.

Your Last DD-214

Your outprocessing team will give you a draft of your final DD-214 during your outprocessing. Make sure you bring any earlier DD-214s and documentation for all your military awards before you go to your final outprocessing. DoD systems do not share information easily with one another and it will be a lot easier for you to make sure any awards or education make it onto your DD-214 if you have a copy of the documentation rather than asking your retirement counselor to take your word for it. Once you leave service, it is incredibly difficult to correct your final DD-214. It is best to arrive to your outprocessing with a well-arranged file that includes all supporting documentation to make sure your last DD-214 has all the right information.

Check to make sure your DD-214 accurately shows your years of service both for CONUS and OCONUS service. If you have Foreign Service documented on an earlier DD-214, that service will not be reflected on your final DD-214. Your final DD-214 only represents any active-duty service you've had since your last DD-214, so don't be surprised if you've changed branches of service (or left active duty and then returned) and don't see your foreign service listed on your last DD-214. Feel free to ask questions when your outprocessing counselor is working with you on the DD-214.

Before you leave the outprocessing station, you will receive two copies of your DD-214. At the bottom of the forms, you will see one form that has "MEMBER-1" and one that has "MEMBER-4." The one marked "MEMBER-4" will have the characterization of your discharge and your separation and re-entry codes. This is the DD-214 you will need when you apply for veterans benefits like a VA loan or a veterans' preference for certain types of employment. Safeguard these documents and store paper and electronic copies in places that are easily accessible.

What's Left at the End

You will receive two copies of your DD-214. Safeguard them. Consider scanning them and keeping electronic copies in several places—like on your computer and in a cloud-based file system. Make sure other members of your family know how to get copies of your DD-214.

You will likely receive a templated letter from your branch of service, thanking you for your service and commending you on the time you spent in uniform. If you are retiring, you—and your spouse—may receive some other templated letters or certificates signed by high-ranking military officials in your branch of service and even the President of the United States. These certificates are great documents to frame and keep in your "me" room.

Some branches will present you with a U.S. flag or a coin when you leave service. As with all things military, whether you will receive them when you outprocess will be subject to funding, supply issues, and availability.

There's No Parade

Seriously, there's no parade. Once you finish completing all the stations, you will have to "sign out" for your "final out." While this sounds formal and solemn, you will likely just wait in a cubicle chair for the office manager. The manager will thank you for your service and will sign (or e-sign) your final outprocessing paperwork. Once everything is signed, you might be handed some additional paperwork or certificates. But after that, you're released. Congratulations!

And that's it. When you leave the office, you will get into your car, buckle your seatbelt, and look around the parking lot for a few minutes thinking about what just happened. You've either finished your required term of service or retired, and it's now over. Prepare for this moment because it's just weird. However, you're not the only one who has gone through it. Make it a point to talk to your close family members about what you're feeling and maybe call a battle buddy once things sink in. In the end, there's no reason you can't throw your own parade, so don't forget the party planning.

ABOUT THE AUTHORS

John J. Wojcik, JD, DBA

Dr. John Wojcik has thirty-two years of military service and retired at the rank of Colonel. His service includes service as a reservist with the Pennsylvania National Guard and the Michigan National Guard. After the September 11th attacks, he left private practice and went on active duty with the Michigan Army National Guard. He served as Judge Advocate and general counsel on active duty for twenty years. In addition to Dr. Wojcik's deployment to Afghanistan, he also served in Liberia and Latvia, where he worked alongside international stakeholders to help the Department of Defense meet its national security objectives. His military awards include the Bronze Star Medal, Meritorious Service Ribbon, Afghanistan Campaign Medal, and the German Armed Forces Badge for Military Proficiency.

Dr. Wojcik was instrumental in forming the Ingham County Veterans Treatment Court in East Lansing, Michigan, and served as Board Chair for both the State of Michigan Retirement Board and Military Law Section for the State Bar of Michigan. He has been an adjunct faculty member at Thomas M. Cooley Law School since 2004. Dr. Wojcik received his BS from the Indiana University of Pennsylvania, JD from Thomas Cooley Law School, and Master of Strategic Studies degree from the U.S. Army War College. He earned his Doctor of Business Administration degree from Baker College where, after eighteen months of research, he defended his dissertation on the hurdles that service members face when they transition from active duty to their first civilian job.

Kimberlie K England, MBA

Kimberlie England spent twelve years as a principal for a regional business consulting firm. She founded Blue Feather Consulting to use her over-twenty years of Human Capital consulting experience to drive strategic change initiatives within varying industries, cultures, and structures.

Kimberlie specializes in leadership coaching, strategic planning, and communication. Her mindful approach to individual and organizational change leads to sustainability. She has successfully led clients into new leadership roles and supported organizations through culture transformations, mergers and acquisitions, and new HR strategies.

Kimberlie received her Executive Coaching certificate from the Weatherhead School of Management at Case Western Reserve University and holds her Board Certified Coach (BCC) certification. She also earned multiple HR certifications including her Professional in Human Resources (PHR), SHRM Certified Professional (SHRM-CP), and Certified Employee Benefits Specialist (CEBS). She received her MBA from the University of Findlay and her BBA from the University of Toledo.

Kimberlie has also volunteered extensively in her community, including serving for over ten years as the Chair of the Human Resources Committee for the Board of Directors of The Ability Center of Greater Toledo. She was instrumental in merging the Assistance Dogs of America into a program of The Ability Center. She is currently a member of the Naval Academy Garden Club and the Naval Academy Spouse's Club in Annapolis, MD.

APPENDIX A

MILITARY ASSOCIATIONS

American Legion

AMVETS

Air Force Association

Association of the United States Army

Disabled American Veterans

Fleet Reserve Association

Marine Corps League

Marine Corps Reserve Association

Marine Executive Association

Marine for Life

Military Officers Association of America

Navy League of the United States

National Guard Association of (Your State)

National Guard Association of the United States

Non-commissioned Officers Association

Reserve Officers Association

U.S. Army Warrant Officers Association

Veterans of Foreign Wars

APPENDIX B

Veterans' Affinity Group Charter

A charter is a written document created to provide direction for the affinity group. The group charter should provide a clear and simple mission that everyone in the group supports. The charter can also be a guide for any activity considered or pursued by the affinity group. This section provides a sample that can get you started on creating a charter for your veterans' affinity group.

GROUP NAME: [ORGANIZATION NAME] VETERANS' AFFINITY GROUP	
SPONSOR NAME	[insert sponsor name]
	The Sponsor's role is to act as a champion and visible representative of the Affinity Group offering visioning advice and a broader perspective of the organization's leadership.
	The sponsor allows the Affinity Group's leaders and members to act independently, but the sponsor must be available for counsel when needed.
	The sponsor will ensure that the Veterans' Affinity Group is given physical space to meet and store materials or supplies that benefit the group.

KEY LEADERS	[insert name], Chair
	[insert name], Vice-Chair
	[insert name], Organizational Liaison
	[insert name], Treasurer
	• All leaders will be employed by [organization name] "in good standing" at the time of election or appointment. Employment in good standing means the individual is not under active disciplinary action.

MISSION STATEMENT

We facilitate the inclusion of veterans, military members, and their families into our organization by supporting recruitment, retention, camaraderie, and ongoing success.

ORGANIZATIONAL NEED	To help veterans, military members, and their families feel more comfortable and learn more about our organization and each other, the [organization name] Veterans' Affinity Group was formed.
	Note: The Veterans' Affinity Group is not intended to represent employees regarding the terms and conditions of employment with [organization name].

ORGANIZATIONAL BENEFITS	• Improve veteran recruitment efforts by connecting veterans to the organization • Increase camaraderie by offering veterans opportunities to network with each other and learn more about the organization • Help build the organization's external reputation through community involvement • Increase morale and retention by engaging veteran employees and providing support, networking, and career development opportunities • Enhance leadership skills of group members through specific programming or events designed to create better leaders at the organization

POLICIES	• The group will be a supported by [organization name] as long as it continues to deliver on its mission statement and provides the defined benefits to the organization.
	• The Affinity Group's activities, programs, and services will not be represented, directly or indirectly, as official functions or activities of [organization name] without prior, written authorization from an authorized role at the organization.
	• The fiscal year of the Affinity Group shall be the same as the Company fiscal year.
	• The group will comply with [organization name] policies and procedures regarding discrimination and harassment in the workplace, and will not discriminate against any member, potential member, or employee.
	• Affinity Groups are encouraged to collaborate with each other and participate in joint activities where appropriate to maximize resources for each group.
	• [Organization name] will provide an annual budget for the group that will be communicated by the Finance Director before the start of each calendar year. There is no guarantee of the amount of each year's annual budget.
	• Members may not receive any compensation from the Affinity Group, except for reimbursement of expenses.
	• Affinity Group members must conduct themselves in a professional manner at all times when participating in group meetings and activities either inside or outside the organization.

MEMBERSHIP	<ul><li>To be a member of the Veterans' Affinity group, you must be a full-time or part-time employee of [company name] who:<ul><li>Has prior military service</li><li>Is active in the National Guard or Reserves</li><li>Has a spouse or parent that is active-duty military</li><li>Has a deep interest in making sure veterans succeed in the workplace</li></ul></li><li>Membership in the group and attendance or participation at any group meetings or activities is voluntary.</li><li>Employees must not be performing normal job duties as part of participation in the Veterans' Affinity Group meetings or activities without prior authorization from [organization name].</li></ul>
COMMITTEES	<ul><li>Communication. Produces member communication as well as managing any website or social media communication.</li><li>Community Relations. Coordinates relationships with other Affinity Groups, and develops partnerships with the external organizations that share a mission with the group.</li><li>Programming. Organizes special events, educational opportunities, and external programming. May also assist onboarding new members.</li><li>Finance. Manages the budget that is provided by the organization. May also be responsible for special fundraising opportunities.</li></ul>

RECORDKEEPING	The Affinity Group needs to keep correct and complete records of its spending and financial transactions. Files must be kept in electronic format using spreadsheets or other financial planning software. The files must be stored as instructed by [organization name] and be accessible for review by the leadership of [organization name]. Examples of commonly requested records include the following:

- Financial summary. Monthly report that captures spending and remaining budget

- Member roster. List of active and non-active members of the Affinity group, which includes contact information

- Event calendar. An annual calendar that shows all the past and upcoming events

- Strategic plan or annual objectives. Report that documents the review of the mission, vision or objectives for the group; planning should be done at least every three years

REFERENCES

Buckland, M. (August 14, 2014). *25 fun facts about resumes, interviews, and social recruitment.* Business 2 Community.

Carter, B. (March 1, 2014). *Can 10,000 hours of practice make you an expert?* BBC News.

Editors (July 12, 2021). *The U.S. military needs a lot more recruits.* Bloomberg Opinion Online.

Guo, C., Pollak, J., and Bauman, M. (2016). *Ten frequently asked questions about veterans' transitions.* Rand Corporation.

Hall, C., Harrell, M., Bicksler, B., Steward, R., and Fisher, M. (2014) *Veteran employment: Lessons from the 100,000 jobs mission.* Rand Corporation.

IDS Water (August 2, 2020). *How much does it cost to send a soldier to basic training?* IDS Water online.

LinkedIn (June 22, 2017). *Eighty-percent of professionals consider networking important to career success.* LinkedIn Corporate Communications.

Maury, R., Stone, B., and Roseman, J. (2014). *Veteran job retention survey summary.* Vet Advisor.

McKee, A., Boyatzis, R., and Johnston, F. (2008). *Becoming a resonant leader.* Harvard Business Press.

Minnis, S. (2014). *A phenomenological exploration of combat veterans' experiences as they transition to civilian employment using higher education as career development.* [Unpublished doctoral dissertation]. Texas A & M University.

Schafer, A., Swick, A, Kiddler, K., and Carter, P. (2016, November). *Onward and upward: Understanding veteran retention and performance in the workforce.* Center for a New American Security.

Society for Human Resource Management (2016). *2016 human capital benchmarking report.*

U.S. Chamber of Commerce Foundation (2016). *Veterans in the workplace. Understanding the challenges and creating long-term opportunities for veteran employees.*

U.S. Department of Defense (2018). *2018 Demographics.*

Williams, R., Allen-Collinson, J., Hockey, J., and Evans, A (2018). "You're just chopped off at the end: Retired servicemen's identity work struggles in the military to civilian transition." *Sociological Research Online.* 23(4).

Wojcik, J. (2021). *Why do officers leave their civilian jobs?* [Doctoral dissertation, Baker College]. Proquest Dissertations.